Embroidered Boxes

Frontispiece: Garden box with base sides in moulded thick card on a base platform. 12 in × 10 in × 3 in (30 cm × 25 cm × 7 cm)

Embroidered Boxes
Making Practical Items for Embroidery

JANE LEMON

with photographs by Valerie Campbell-Harding
and Rob Matheson

B.T. BATSFORD LTD · LONDON

ISBN 0 7134 4587 4

Printed in Great Britain by
Courier International Ltd, Tiptree, Essex
for the Publishers
B.T. Batsford Ltd
4 Fitzhardinge Street
London W1H 0AH

Originally published by Faber and Faber Ltd as Embroidered Boxes and Other
Construction Techniques. © Jane Lemon 1980

The front cover photograph shows a 'stained glass window box', in black gloving suede laced
over thick card to show varied colours of silks laid behind. $11\frac{1}{2}$ in $\times$ $11\frac{1}{2}$ in $\times$ 4 in
(29 cm $\times$ 29 cm $\times$ 10 cm).

Contents

List of Illustrations

Acknowledgements

My gratitude goes to Valerie Harding and Jan Messent without whose persuasion, continual support and encouragement this book would never have come about.

My deepest thanks to Valerie Harding for all her time and effort given to the photographs that play such a major part in the book.

I should like to thank Kathleen Anderson, Joan Broughton, Diana Browne, Midge Burnett, Dorothy Carbonell, Audrey Chorley, Mollie Collins, Eileen Cottle, Valda Cowie, Eleanor Fielden, Trotman Foster, Sara Getley, Mary Greening, Valerie Harding, Lois Hennequin, Lucy Judd, Diana Keay, Molly Lance, Mid-Wessex Branch of the Embroiderers' Guild, Belinda Montagu, Beryl Morgan, Daphne Nicholson, Mollie Picken, Susan Rangeley, Mollie Ruthven and Pamela Watts for allowing me to photograph their work. The pieces that are not acknowledged are my own.

Anne Dyer for her work on the glossary.

Diana Keay for her help in finding bag shapes.

Mary Platt for sharing her experience with blinds.

Jane Pearce and Esme Shaw for their endless typing.

Sarah Gleadell and Julia Lilauwala for their patience and hard work as my editor and designer.

My husband and my family for their understanding and help in getting this book completed.

Lastly, my thanks are due to E. K. Norris without whom I would never have taken up embroidery.

Introduction

Embroiderers are becoming more and more interested in ways of putting the work on which they have spent so much time and effort to practical use, but many do not have the specialized knowledge needed to do this successfully. Boxes in particular are an increasingly popular medium for the display of fine embroidery and, although not intrinsically difficult to make, they do require a certain basic understanding of construction techniques. This book contains a complete breakdown of the techniques for making a wide variety of boxes and their fittings, as well as describing the construction of many types of bags and purses, cushions, curtains, blinds and book covers.

I very much hope that *Embroidered Boxes* will help embroiderers to achieve a really professional finish in all the articles they choose to make. What it cannot provide is the last vital ingredient—time. I too have been caught the day before an event or exhibition with the last stages of construction still to complete, so I understand the problem only too well.

When I first worked in the theatre in a workroom making costumes for Sadler's Wells Theatre Ballet Company, the cutter in charge was Andy, an expert in her field and a marvellous personality. She was one of the most generous people I have ever met in passing on her wealth of knowledge to her young machinists. When we were working under real pressure for a first night, one of us would say, 'I've nearly finished this costume, I've only got the hem and . . .', Andy would interrupt and say, 'I know, you've got ninety-nine more hours to do!'

Please, do give yourself those precious ninety-nine more hours to complete the piece, and do justice to your craft and to yourself.

CHAPTER ONE

General Construction

Enlarging Patterns and Designs

Take the drawing, photograph or pattern that you want to enlarge and divide it up into squares. The more detail that is required, the smaller the squares will need to be.

For a pattern of a purse or bag, 1-in (3-cm) squares are usually small enough. For a design of postcard size, ½-in (1-cm) squares should be sufficiently small. This will give 11 squares by 7 squares if worked in inches (14 squares by 9 squares in centimetres) (Fig. 1).

Take a piece of paper and place the postcard on the bottom left-hand corner. Mark the width that is required for the enlargement on the bottom edge of the paper and with a set square draw a perpendicular line towards the top of the paper. Next draw a line from the bottom left-hand corners of the postcard and paper, through the top right-hand corner of the postcard and continue it until it cuts the perpendicular from the base line. This gives the height of your enlargement. Draw a line from this point parallel to the base line to meet the left-hand edge of the paper (Fig. 2).

The base line of the enlargement now has to be divided up to give the same number of squares as the base line of the postcard; the vertical lines are similarly divided. Lines are ruled up and across to form squares, using a set square for accuracy.

Having prepared the enlarged grid, it is now possible to mark points of the design or pattern in each square, or where the design crosses a line from the postcard grid. These points are then joined up, giving the enlarged design (Fig. 3).

Blocking or Stretching the Embroidery

Never use an iron on a piece of embroidery as it flattens the textural quality. Many pieces of work, especially canvas-work, will need to be stretched to return the work to its true shape, having been distorted in the working. Stretching also smooths out the threads to give a pressed appearance without flattening the stitchery.

A flat wooden board is needed, slightly larger than the work. Onto this is laid a well-dampened folded sheet or several wet layers of white blotting paper. Canvas-work is laid face down onto this damp surface, so that the back of the canvas can be additionally damped with a sponge. All other types of embroidery are laid with the right side uppermost, as sufficient dampness will seep through from the back. As the work dampens, it becomes pliable and can easily be stretched tight and into shape.

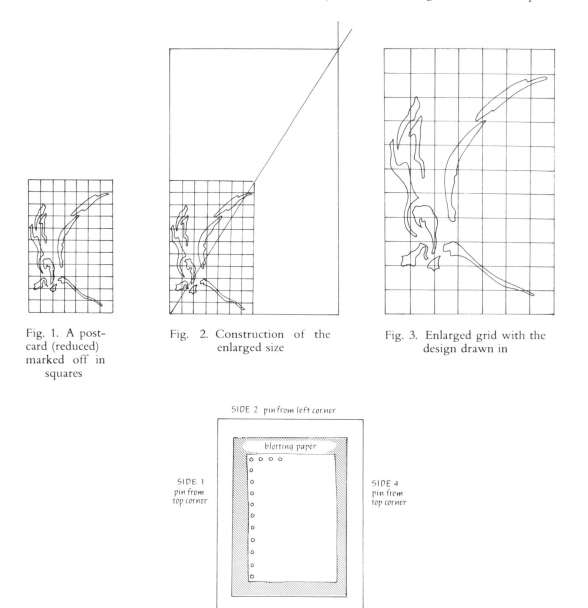

Fig. 1. A post-card (reduced) marked off in squares

Fig. 2. Construction of the enlarged size

Fig. 3. Enlarged grid with the design drawn in

Fig. 4. Blocking the embroidery

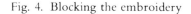

A straight edge of the work is pinned down at $\frac{1}{2}$-inch (15-mm) intervals with brass drawing pins (thumb tacks) through the unworked turnings of the embroidery, parallel to the edge of the board. Having pinned one side, continue round the corner, pulling gently and pinning the second side at right angles to the first, again parallel to the edge of the board. Continue round the four sides, stretching and pinning the embroidery into shape (Fig. 4). The work needs to be left for a couple of days to dry out completely, when it will be ready for mounting or making up. It is always a surprise how much more professional the work looks after stretching.

Cutting Card

The weight of card used for construction in mounting embroidery very much depends on the size and type of article that is being made. Individual types of card are listed under the different chapter headings. The art of cutting card accurately and cleanly is the same technique in all cases. Naturally, the thicker the card, the more difficult it is to cut, but there are one or two hints which should help to make it easier.

A good sharp knife is essential, and a Stanley knife with a retractable blade is to be recommended. So many craft knives are excellent for other purposes, but not heavy enough to cut the mill-board type of card.

Accurately cut card is of the foremost importance to a crisp, well-made box or any other constructed object. If the angles are inaccurate at this preliminary stage, there is nothing that can be done to correct them later. Use a hard, sharp pencil that gives a clean line, a set square for accurate right angles and a steel rule for cutting against.

Having drawn a line to be cut, it will be found that the sharp pencil has made an indenture on the card. The blade of the knife can be set in this and gently drawn along to score the surface. This is easy enough on a straight line when the knife can be used against the ruler, but on a curved line when it often has to be done freehand, it is vital to cut a single correct line with no snicks to left or right. Having scored the surface, however lightly, the knife will stay in this track and weight can be applied to cut right through the card on the second time round. When cutting card, the knife needs to be angled to use as much of the cutting edge as possible, not just the point (Fig. 5). The cut edge of the card will then need to be smoothed off with a fine grade sandpaper to give a good finish.

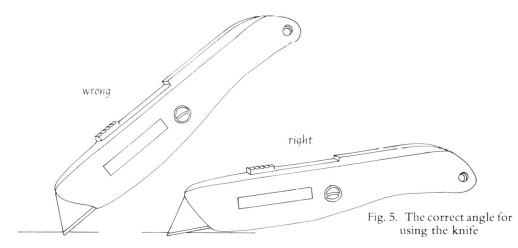

wrong

right

Fig. 5. The correct angle for using the knife

Grain

When designing a piece of work, it is important to plan where the straight grain will lie. Very often it will run north–south straight through the centre of the work, and it is vital that it is cut absolutely accurately, as a slope of even $\frac{1}{4}$ in (5 mm) off centre will give the illusion of the whole piece being uneven or lopsided. Care must also be taken to cut the pieces of fabric from the same direction of the warp and weft of the material. Most people are aware of the variation of colour, light and shade in velvet, but this is also true of the majority of modern fabrics, where many also have a strong directional weave on the weft. It is important that this textural line is planned with the embroidery so that they compliment each other; the rest of the article is cut to match. Omission of these details can completely wreck an otherwise well-made article.

Material cut on the cross or a bias strip is needed at certain times when more stretch is required, and the fabric needed to mould itself round a surface without pleating or wrinkling. This cannot be achieved unless the crossway piece is accurately cut (Fig. 6).

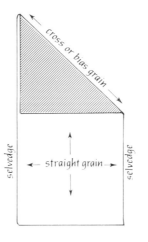

Fig. 6. Cutting a crossway strip

Treatment of Fraying Edges

Many fabrics fray very badly and need treating before handling in any way. Where there are turnings, this can be done by medium-sized zig-zagging on the sewing machine or oversewing by hand. Canvas is more easily worked if the raw edges are bound with tape, so that the working yarns don't catch on the stiff threads every time a stitch is made.

Where the fabric is being cut to shape for appliqué, a self-adhesive fabric stiffener can be ironed onto the back before the shape is cut out. This will hold the edges firm whilst it is being applied and the edges treated more permanently. If the fabric is very fine, like a silk, the iron-on fabric stiffener can give an adverse effect by giving the fabric a hard, stiff quality which spoils it. In this case, a line of clear nail varnish painted on the line of the shape before cutting it will stop the threads from fraying.

For small pieces of appliqué or three-dimensional work, the entire piece of material can be painted with a weak solution of clear gum and water and allowed to dry before the required shapes are cut out. This also gives the smaller pieces a certain amount of stiffness, which makes them easier to handle.

Use of Glue

Although I advocate glue in the above case, very little glue is needed in the actual construction of an article, except if it is being made of leather. There is no advantage in glueing fabric over card instead of lacing. More often than not, the glue marks the fabric somewhere; and it is possible to lace in less time than the glue takes to dry, usually with a crisper result. However, a little glue is sometimes useful to flatten a mitred corner when lacing over card or to hold wadding or felt in position on the card.

The best glues to use are millinery rubber solution, which is not always easily available, and white, water-based school glue, which can be bought in large stationers and art shops. There is a spray glue and a glue made up into a stick, both of which are excellent, but very much more expensive.

When cutting wadding and felt to the size of a piece of card, it is much more accurate to spread glue thinly onto the prepared card and then lay this onto the uncut length of wadding or felt. Having smoothed out the padding so that it is stretched over the card, it is then very easy to trim it accurately to size (Fig. 7). If the wadding or felt is cut to size first and then glued into position on the card, it will be found that it is nearly always too large and has to be retrimmed, or worse that it shrinks back from the edges of the card and is too small!

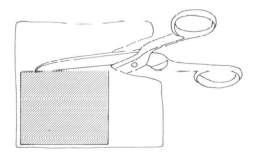

Fig. 7. Trimming the surplus felt away from the glued cardboard

Mitred Corners

When lacing fabric over card, mitred corners are the neatest, flattest method of covering a corner. Due to the thickness of the card, it is not possible to get as perfectly mitred a corner as one can using a piece of flat linen on the corner of a tray cloth, but it is adequate, tidy and keeps the fabric firmly in position. As it is always hidden within the construction of the article, flatness is of prime importance, rather than achieving the perfect mitred corner (Fig. 8).

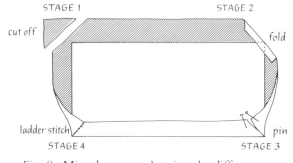

Fig. 8. Mitred corners showing the different stages

Lacing

In order to cover card with fabric, it is necessary to lace it into position. First of all lay the card onto the wrong side of the fabric with the edge of the card lying on either the straight grain of the fabric, or the true cross, whichever the design demands. The fabric is then pinned into position from the right side by pressing a pin through the fabric into the edge of the card (Fig. 9). The mitred corners are then pinned into position (Fig. 8) and sewn with a matching thread. Lacing may now begin. A strong thread is needed for this, otherwise it is easily snapped as the work is tightened. Linen thread is ideal, but unfortunately this is hardly obtainable now and far too expensive for this use. A fine crochet cotton does the job extremely well and is easily available. The thread is taken from side to side of the card, taking a $\frac{3}{8}$-in (5-mm) stitch well into the turning of the fabric, so that it does not fray out (Fig. 10). In order that the lacing thread remains taut and does not slacken back on itself, it is a great help to make a half-hitch or buttonhole stitch on every third or fourth stitch. Having laced the fabric into position in one direction, lace it at right angles to complete the process (Fig. 11).

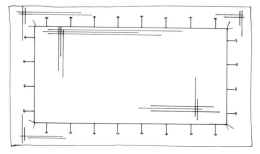

Fig. 9. Fabric covering the card is pinned into position with the grain parallel to the edge of the card

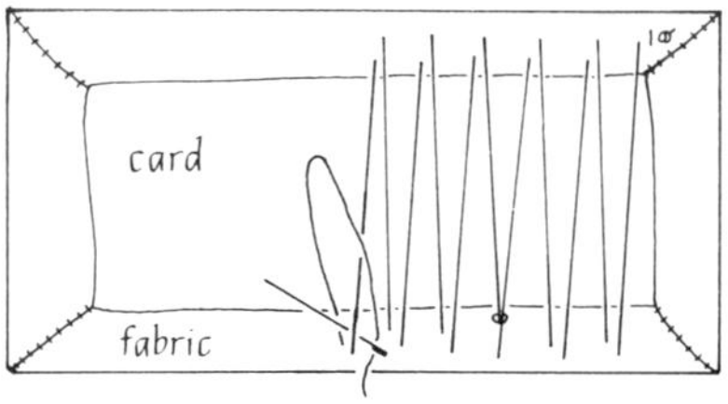

Fig. 10. Lacing the card. Showing buttonhole knot on every third or fourth stitch so tension does not slacken as next stitch is laced

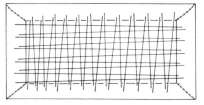

Fig. 11. Lacing completed in both directions

In order not to waste lacing thread, especially on large articles, it is perfectly satisfactory to knot a new length of thread onto the short end, rather than finishing the old end off in the fabric turning and then starting again with a new length in the normal way.

Ladder-Stitch

Ladder-stitch is the method of stitching two pieces together on the right side almost invisibly.

On soft fabric or knitting, the needle picks up the fold on the edge of the seam line. As long as the stitch between the folds is at right angles to the fabric, the thread will be invisible when it is pulled tight (Fig. 12).

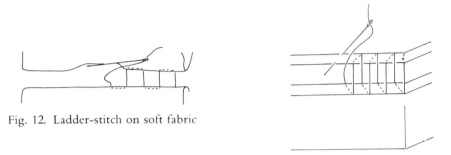

Fig. 12. Ladder-stitch on soft fabric

Fig. 13. Ladder-stitching two hard edges of a box together

On a hard edge, as in boxes, it is stronger if the needle picks up the fold at a slight angle. In this way, several threads of warp and weft are picked up and the material is less likely to rip when the thread is tightened (Fig. 13). It is essential to keep the stitch between the two sections of the box at right angles to the seam.

CHAPTER TWO

Boxes

Designing the Box

It is very important to decide at this early stage what the box will be used for, as it not only has to be a suitable size and shape, but made of the right type of fabric for the amount of wear and tear that it will have to stand up to. In the same way, the selected embroidery technique must be suitable for the chosen fabric and the use of the box. The weight of the material must also be right for the size of the box; a tiny box of heavy tweed would look very clumsy, whilst a very fine silk on a large box would never stand up to the weight of its construction. A box in everyday use for containing pencils or sewing obviously does not require the richness and embellishments that might be suitable for a jewellery box, which is not handled so much.

For the first box being made, it is probably as well to plan that it should only have embroidery on the top of the lid, but once the construction is understood, embroidery can be worked on the sides of the box as well, either as separate units, a continuous border pattern or the lid design continuing on over the edges and down the sides. It is also worth thinking out how the box will be held and opened, so that delicate embroidery like gold-work is not automatically handled when the box is picked up. Similarly, if a white or pastel coloured fabric is chosen, it does help to keep the box clean if definite handles, embroidered leather area or other suitable ideas are thought up to enable the box to be lifted and opened without touching the delicate material, which is bound to get dirty with fingering.

The proportions of the box are very much influenced by the type of lid selected. There are two lids with lips; the overlapping lid (Fig. 32, page 47) and the flush lid with a rising lining (Fig. 41, page 51). The top of the lid normally sits right on top of the lip itself (Fig. 34, page 47), but can be set into the lip which forms a frame (Fig. 35, page 47) if this is more suitable to the general design.

There are three lids without lips; the drop-in lid (Fig. 42, page 51), the pop-on lid (Fig. 43, page 54) and the hinged lid (Fig. 44, page 54).

The various types of lid need to be carefully studied before completing the design for the box.

Plain materials are obviously the simplest to use as there is only the textural weave to consider. In a great number of modern fabrics, this is very strong and must be planned for in the overall design.

A box should be of a balanced design that can be viewed from any angle, but there is nearly always a preferred way for it to stand. If the box is rectangular then usually one thinks of the front as being one of the long sides. It is therefore necessary to decide if this textural stripe should run parallel to the long sides, or from back to front, parallel to the short sides. The embroidery design will influence this decision, as will the general proportions of the box.

If the stripe runs left to right across the box, then it is less disturbing to the eye if this strong weave runs round the base in the same direction (Fig. 14). If, on the other hand, the stripe runs from back to front on the lid, then it needs to run up and down on the sides (Fig. 15).

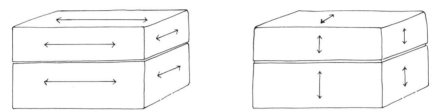

Fig. 14 and Fig. 15. Direction of textural stripe

When a patterned material is chosen, it very often determines the exact dimensions and shape of the box, so that the printed design becomes incorporated and makes a well-designed whole. The sides of the base and the lip of the lid are ideally each cut in one long piece of fabric. This means that there is only one join, which can be set at the so-called back of the box (Fig. 16). Should there be a shortage of fabric, then there can be a join on the other back corner as well. This means that all the other sides are cut in one piece of fabric and the one back side is a separate piece (Fig. 17).

Never have joins on three corners. It is better to have joins on all four corners (Figs 18 and 19).

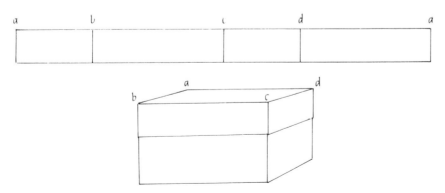

Fig. 16. The long strip forming the lip with one join at the back corner (a)

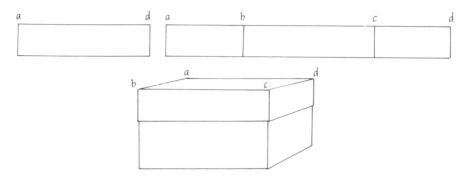

Fig. 17. Showing two joins on the back of the box, with the two short sides and the front long side made up as one piece

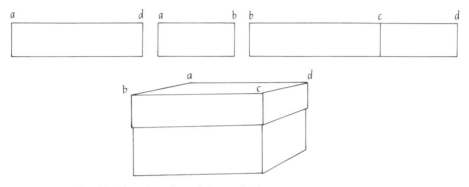

Fig. 18. Showing three joins, which gives a very untidy finish

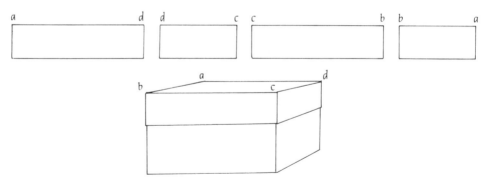

Fig. 19. Showing four joins

When using patterned fabric, it is advisable to have joins on each corner as it is extremely difficult to get the tension exactly right in lacing and keep the pattern positioned accurately on all corners. It is easier to lace each side separately and then ladder-stitch them into position.

In the same way, if the fabric for all the sides is machined together with plans for lacing it as one long strip to give machined joins on each corner, it is practically impossible to achieve as all fabrics need lacing at different tensions to give a satisfactory tight finish. It is very difficult to estimate the correct measurements and end up with the sides laced and the machined joins neatly on each corner.

I like cords on boxes only as an integral part of the design. When cording is laid upon seams my immediate reaction is that it must be hiding a poor bit of stitching. There are very few boxes that are improved in their design by a cord on their seams. Cord softens and rounds off the edge, losing the crispness that is so admired in a well-made box.

The amount of padding used on the outside and inside of the box depends on what it is going to be used for. Inside the box padding gives a protective surface for jewellery and delicate objects. On the outside it gives a richness that is not always necessary. However, even a crisply tailored box will need a thin layer of felt or some material of similar weight, to prevent the card giving the fabric a hard, thin quality.

The design of some boxes is enhanced by feet raising the box off the surface (Plate 26, page 81). Brass and chrome metal studs with split pins for fixing them are obtainable from saddlers and many old-fashioned cobblers. The studs come in a variety of shapes and can be seen on the black leather jackets of some young motor-cyclists.

1 Mid-Wessex box with gold-work design depicting Wiltshire wild fruits: sycamore, hazelnuts, hips, acorns, spindle and blackberry. 20 in × 12 in × 4½ in (51 cm × 30 cm × 12 cm). *Members of the Mid-Wessex Branch of the Embroiderers' Guild*

Holes are made in the base at this stage with a stiletto. The split pins can then be passed through the fabric, felt and card from the outside and splayed tightly open. The lining will then cover up the inside. Make sure that the feet are equidistantly placed from the corner and both sides.

2 Mid-Wessex box open to show the tray with covered compartments

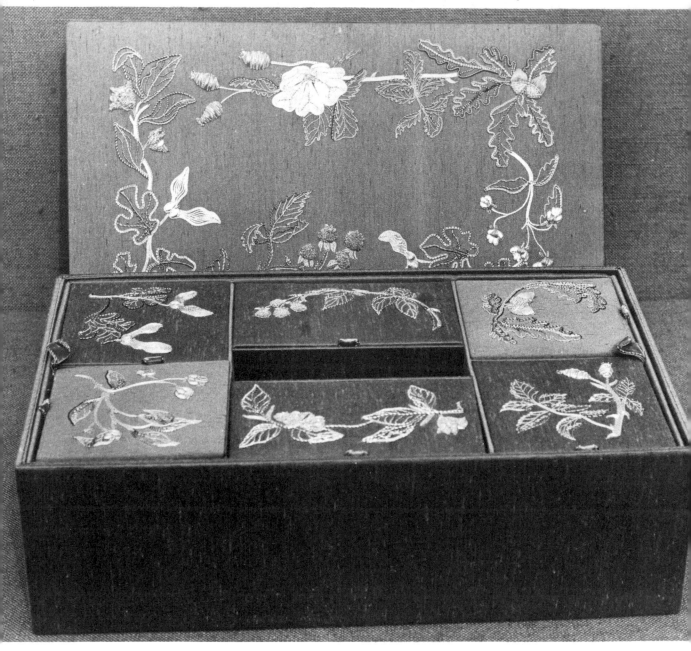

3 Mid-Wessex box with tray removed showing tray supports in the box base

Having planned the general size, shape and outside treatment of the box, it is important to give the same consideration to the interior. Half the fun of boxes is the surprise of finding what is inside (Plates 2 and 3). The outside is constantly being seen, so great detail of embroidery is needed to keep the eye intrigued. The opening of the box should be a sharp surprise, with contrasting colour and fabric used for the lining. Small details of embroidery can be used on compartment lids or quilting for the lining of the lid. The entire lining can be quilted, giving an echo of the outside embroidered design in a different technique, but bear in mind that the contents of the box will hide a great deal of the lining most of the time.

The divisions, compartments, pockets, etc. can be tailor-made for the use of the box and for its future owner. It is always these extra touches that add to the pleasure a box can give. A workbox, with its pockets and slots for tools in the lid lining (Plates 4 and 5) is enormously added to by a matching set of cases for needles, scissors and thimble. A jewellery box for a young girl who collects rings and chooses only chains and long beads, needs to be of a totally different shape (Plate 15, page 65) to the one made for her mother, who has a large number of brooches (Plate 7, page 37).

It is this individuality which adds to the fun of box making.

4 Hinged lid workbox in patterned curtain fabric. 9 in × 9 in × 3½ in (23 cm × 23 cm × 9 cm)

Tools and Materials

Boxes are made from various weights of card suitable to their size and the part that each piece plays in the construction. Each piece of card is laced with fabric and then ladder-stitched together in its correct position.

Card
Mill-board or straw board is a heavy grade grey card which I use for all the main pieces of the box. However, if the overall length of a box exceeds 15 in (37 cm) this card will whip or feel pliable and thicker board is needed. Then hardboard is excellent and makes very good boxes. The only snag is that it cannot be cut with a Stanley knife and has to be sawn. If outside help is needed to do this, it is a definite problem, as I believe that the card or board must be measured and cut as one goes, and not all the pieces cut at the outset. There is too much variation in the thickness of the various fabrics and paddings used to make hard and fast rules about measurements. Therefore one must construct each section of the box, then use it to measure and cut the card for the next part.

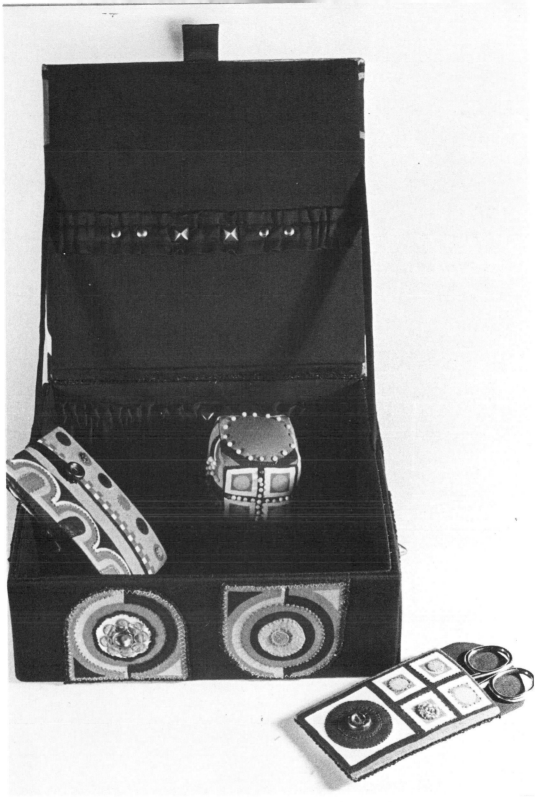

5 Workbox open to show fittings and accessories

Straw board or thick card is used for all sections that are part of the main construction and take any weight, i.e. the base, sides, rising linings, internal partitions, base and sides of a tray, top of the lid, lip of the lid and some lid linings. This will give the necessary firmness to each part.

A thinner card, such as that used for cereal packets, is ideal where no weight is involved, such as linings to the bottom half of the box and most lid linings. As the box takes shape it becomes obvious where heavy card is needed and where it is unnecessary.

For a box of over 15 in (37 cm) length, extra strength can be given to the construction by using thick card throughout, including the lining, thus avoiding the use of hardboard and the difficulty of cutting it. It can make the walls rather thick, which would be too bulky in certain cases. Even this would not be strong enough for the largest boxes. The Mid-Wessex box (20 by 12 in, 50 by 30 cm) (Colour plate F and Plates 1–3) was hardboard lined with thick card.

It does not matter what type of card is used as long as it has enough rigidity for its purpose. There are some very good types of card available in shops selling artists' materials, usually with treated and coloured facings, but they are too expensive to be bought specially. Off-cuts that are to hand can certainly be used. The only type of card that must not be used under any circumstances is that which is used for certain grocery cartons and has a corrugated centre. Although this appears strong, it is quite unsuitable for this purpose.

Tools

It is essential to use a good ruler, preferably a steel one, a set square and a well-sharpened pencil for drawing out the pieces on the sheet of card (see page 21). A Stanley knife is the best instrument for cutting, and fine sandpaper is needed for cleaning off the cut edge before covering.

It is advisable to cut out the card on a large wooden board or a sheet of hardboard, as it is very easy to cut through the card and damage the table before one realizes it.

A compass will be needed for round boxes (Plate 6); it is quicker and more accurate than using a plate or bowl to give a circular template. However, a pie-dish can be very useful if an oval shape is required.

Needles

Normal sewing needles are used, suitable for the size of thread and the fabric being handled. There are cases where a curved needle is most helpful and it is necessary to buy a fine curved mattress needle from an upholstery firm. These are 3 in (7 cm) long and are far easier to handle than the shorter needles sold in commercial packs on the haberdashery counter. Size 22 is very suitable, being fine and sharp.

Glue

A little glue is needed to hold the felt or wadding in position whilst the lacing is being done and both millinery rubber solution and water-based school glue are very good for this purpose. Only very little should be used, so that there is no risk of the glue working through the padding and staining the fabric. Stick-type glue and spray glue avoid this hazard, but they are more expensive (page 23).

6 Two stud boxes based on cardboard tubes of approximately 3 in (7 cm) diameter, the left hand one with a pop-on lid and the right hand one with an overlapping lid

Pins and Clips

Glass-headed pins are much the easiest to use, and kinder on the fingers, as they have to be pushed through the fabric into the edge of the card.

Very large paperclips, clothes pegs and metal bulldog clips are all useful for holding the fabric in position on the card, or for controlling the card when round boxes are being made. When clipping fabric over card, be careful to insert a piece of paper between the clip and the fabric to avoid marking it. This is especially important on leathers (Fig. 20).

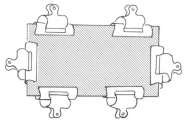

Fig. 20. Leather covered card held by bulldog clips over paper whilst the glue dries

Threads

The thread must, of course, match the fabric. Synthetic threads are preferable to cotton as they have more stretch in them and seem easier to tighten up without snapping.

On fine silks or silk-type fabrics where stitching would show, use nylon invisible thread, which comes in 'clear' or 'smoky' for pale or dark fabrics. This thread takes a little time to get used to, but it is well worth the effort as the results are excellent. It is more amenable if it is waxed before use. To avoid the needle becoming constantly unthreaded, knot the thread onto the eye of the needle. Once this is done it can be handled in the normal way, but be gently firm with it and avoid sudden jerks, which may snap it.

For lacing fabric over card, a heavier thread is needed. Linen thread is ideal but it is too expensive and a fine crochet cotton is an excellent replacement.

Paddings

To prevent the hardness of the card showing through the material, some sort of padding is necessary, except with the thicker, heavier cloths.

Felt gives a really good tailored finish, but it can certainly be substituted by something like off-cuts of flannel out of the rag-bag.

Foam rubber of varying thicknesses, $\frac{1}{8}-\frac{3}{4}$ in (3–20 mm), gives very good results.

There are a number of waddings on the market and any of them can be used, but the easiest to handle is that made of Courtelle. It is sold in various weights, but can easily be split down to the thickness required for each individual box. The fact that it is a synthetic fibre makes it washable, easier to handle and less likely to disintegrate.

Wadding or thicker foam is used for the richer padded areas. How thick it needs to be depends on the fabric that will cover it, the size and the use of the box.

Fabric

The fabric needs to be of a close weave and strong enough for the size of box being made. If it is too thin the padding will show through; if it is too thick it will look clumsy.

For boxes with corners it is inadvisable to use a stretchy fabric like Courtelle, jersey or a panné velvet, as the corners are difficult to control. However, on a circular or oval box, this stretchiness is an asset and can avoid the necessity of cutting the fabric on the cross to get a good smooth finish.

Leather can make beautiful boxes; obviously the thinner skins are the easiest to handle. The methods are the same as for fabric, but I do glue the leather to the back of the card instead of lacing. This means that the leather must be pinned, or clipped with bulldog clips over paper to avoid marking, while it dries, to make sure that it is really stretched tight (Fig. 20, page 36), and enough time allowed for it to be really firm before the next stage is worked. Apart from this, everything is ladder-stitched together as with the other boxes. Stitches of less than $\frac{1}{8}$ in (3 mm) can cause the leather to split, so it is advisable to keep the stitches a little larger than on fabric boxes. Use an ordinary needle and proceed as for fabric.

PATTERNED FABRIC Small repeat patterns can be charming either for the outside or the inside of the box. Larger patterns must be centred up within the shapes of the box sections. This means that the pattern, especially with geometric designs, will determine the size of the box (Plates 7 and 8).

7 Indian box open to show tray and compartments for jewellery

8 Indian box with a flush lid and rising lining. Each corner has joins because of the patterned fabric. 12 in × 9 in × 5 in (30 cm × 23 cm × 13 cm). Small round box fixed to the lid takes up the circular design on the fabric. 6 in diameter × 2½ in high (15 cm diameter × 6 cm high)

Order of Work

This résumé is intended to help with the making of boxes, but it is essential to have read the detailed methods and techniques in the following sections before enthusiastically cutting the first box.

   The box is built up from the base in much the same order as building a house. It is essential to complete each stage before measuring for the next part. This means that it is inadvisable to cut all the card at the beginning, as it may well be wrong when the relevant stage of construction is reached.

1. Plan use, size, shape, embroidery and fabric for the outside and the lining.
2. Check that there is enough main fabric for base, base sides, lip of lid if there is one, and top of lid.

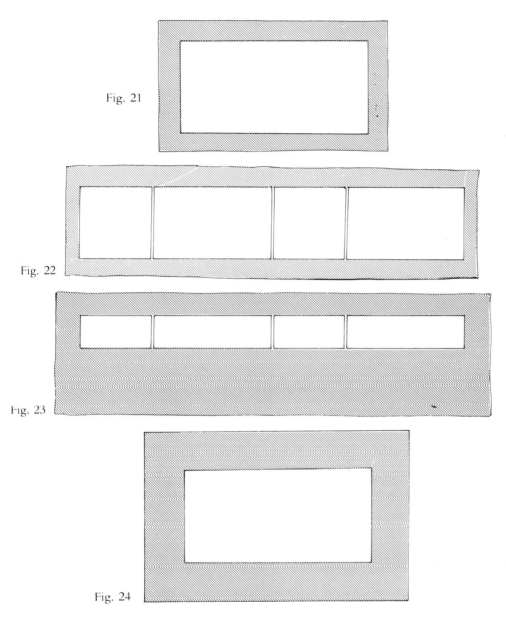

Fig. 21

Fig. 22

Fig. 23

Fig. 24

Base Measurement of card plus 1½-in (4-cm) turnings all round (Fig. 21).
Sides Length of card plus turnings all round (Fig. 22).
Lip of lid Length of card plus turnings at each end. Twice the width of card plus at least 2 in (5 cm) for turnings (Fig. 23).
Lid Measurement of card plus good turnings all round. The top of the lid is often as much as ½ in (15 mm) bigger than the base in length and width.
Extra turnings are needed for a pop-on lid and a hinged lid where the linings are smaller than for the usual lids (Fig. 24).

The bottom of the box can be of a different fabric, as long as it tones in colour and is a suitable choice to mix with the side material. It is rarely seen and it is a pity to spoil a whole concept for a box because of a shortage of the chosen material.

3. Cut out fabric and work the embroidered areas. If the sides of the box are being embroidered, it is essential to construct the base first and Scotch-tape the padded card sides into position before measuring round the box to get the length of fabric required. This is because the embroidery, especially if it had been framed up and backed with calico, will have no stretch. The measurement going round the card in its proper position on the base is substantially larger than when the card is laid flat end to end. When plain fabric is used there is enough stretch to cater for this, but it must be allowed for when the sides are being embroidered. The same applies for an embroidered lip of a lid.

4. Cut base in thick card, pad with felt and lace with fabric.
   If a drop-in lid is being made, cut card for top of lid exactly the same as the base card (Fig. 42, page 51).
   If it is a flush-sided box with top of lid being framed by lip, then cut the card for the top of lid exactly the same as the base card (Fig. 35, page 47).

5. Use covered base to measure thick card for base sides (Fig. 26, page 43).

6. Cut base sides in thick card. Pad as required (Fig. 7, page 23). Lace with fabric (Fig. 10, page 24).
   For a flush-sided box, cut pieces of card for lip of lid exactly the same length as the card for base sides, but with less depth. The depth of the sides and the lip will have been decided in the design.

7. Join base sides to form box with ladder-stitch (Fig. 13, page 25).

8. Push the sides over the base. Pin and ladder-stitch (Fig. 29, page 44).

9. Using the base sides, measure thick card for overlapping lip.

10. Cut thick card for overlapping lip, pad and cover with fabric (Fig. 36, page 49). Join up with ladder-stitch.

11. Place overlapping lip into position on the base and use it to measure for the normal lid that will lie on top of lip.
    If the top of the lid is to be framed by the lip, then the measurement will be that of the covered base sides.

12. For a pop-on lid or a hinged lid, use the sides of the base to measure for the lid, which will lie on the top (Figs. 43, 44, page 54). In some cases, these will extend by $\frac{1}{4}$ in (5 mm) or more all round the box to give a finger grip for lifting and a design interest.

13. Cut thick card for top of lid, pad as required and lace on fabric. Ladder-stitch lip to lid where necessary.

14. Cut lining to lid.
    Overlapping lid and flush-sided lid Thin card to fit neatly up to the inside of the lip. Pad and lace on the fabric. Sew into position.
    Drop-in lid Thin card cut $\frac{1}{8}$ in (3 mm) smaller than the lid all round. Pad, lace on the fabric and ladder-stitch onto lid.

Pop-on lid Thick card cut a fraction smaller than the interior measurement of the box, so that when the card is covered, it will be a snug fit. This lining cannot be measured until the side linings of the base are inserted.

Hinged lid Thin card as for drop-in lid.

15. Cut lining for bottom of box in thin card, pad and lace with lining fabric.

16. Cut side linings for base of box in thin card, except for a box with a rising lining (Fig. 41, page 51), where thick card is necessary.

    The height of the linings for different lids is as follows:

    Flush-sided lid Lining projects above the base sides, not more than $\frac{1}{2}$ in (15 mm) less than the depth of the lip.

    Drop-in lid Lining can be either thin or thick card and as the lid rests on it, needs to be $\frac{1}{4}$ in (5 mm) below the sides of the base.

    Pop-on lid Lining should be level with the base sides.

    Hinged lid As pop-on lid.

    Overlapping lid As pop-on lid.

    Pad and lace with fabric. Join into shape.

17. Sew base lining to side linings if compartments are being made.

18. Cut thick card for compartments, divisions and tray supports where required.

19. Make-up compartments, divisions and tray supports by padding, lacing or covering with fabric (Fig. 70, page 63) on both sides as required.

20. *Tray* Cut sides in thick card. Pad on inside only. Cover as for lip (Fig. 36, page 49), and ladder-stitch into shape.

    Cut thick card for tray base to fit inside the sides, allowing room for fabric to be laced. Pad with felt on the underside, cover with fabric and lace.

    Make long strip for handles, insert (Fig. 25), ladder-stitch base into sides fixing in the handles. Cut base lining in thin card, pad and lace fabric. Drop in and attach, using the same method as attaching a lining of a lid with lip (page 51).

Fig. 25. Inserting a long strip to make handles for a tray

Rectangular and Square Boxes

Having planned the size and the proportions of the box, chosen the materials suitable for its purpose and designed the embroidered areas, a start can be made on the construction.

Base

Measure out the base on thick card using a sharp pencil, set square and, preferably, a steel rule. It is essential to be accurate at this stage, as any faults will only be accentuated as the work proceeds.

Cut the card with a Stanley knife, using a cutting board underneath the card to prevent damage to the table. (See GENERAL CONSTRUCTION, cutting card, page 21.)

The cut edges of the card will need to be smoothed off with fine sandpaper.

If the box being made has either a drop-in lid, or is a flush-sided box with the top of the lid set into the lip of the lid, the top of the lid should be cut at this stage in thick card, exactly the same size as the base card.

PADDING BASE Unless the fabric being used is a thick wool, tweed or leather, a thin padding is needed on the base of the box. Felt or similar weight fabric is the most suitable as it is firm, whereas a thin wadding or foam rubber will not sit flat and will have a bouncy quality which is unsuitable for the base of a box. Having padded the card for the base, make sure that no glue has seeped through the felt. If so, let it dry out completely and use less glue next time.

COVERING BASE Cut out the fabric for the base with 1½-in (4-cm) turnings (Fig. 21, page 39) being careful to cut on the straight grain. Too little turning can be a nuisance if it frays; too much gets in the way and adds needless bulk, so keep the turnings as small as can be easily handled.

Lay the fabric onto the felted side of the base card and check that the grain runs parallel to the edge of the card. Stick pins at 1-in (3-cm) intervals through the fabric and into the edge of the card (Fig. 9, page 24). By doing this the fabric is kept really taut and on the straight grain while the corners are being mitred and the fabric is laced on the wrong side.

Turn the card over so that the wrong side is uppermost and pin all four mitres into position. Sew them off in turn using a matching coloured thread (Fig. 8, page 24). Due to the thickness of the card, it is impossible to get a perfect mitre, but cut away any surplus turnings and keep everything as flat as possible. I personally find that it is easier to mitre the corners before lacing the fabric, though I know that a lot of people do lace first then mitre the corners.

Next lace the fabric in both directions, using a fine crochet cotton or similar-weight linen thread. The important thing is that the thread should not have any stretch in it, otherwise it is difficult to maintain the tension required on the fabric. Begin with a knot and a back-stitch and take long stitches from top to bottom across the back of the card. After every third or fourth long stitch, it helps if a buttonhole stitch or half hitch is taken on the lacing. This knot prevents the thread slackening whilst working (Fig. 10, page 24). Having laced the full length of the base from top to bottom, repeat with lacing from side to side at right angles.

Sides

Cut the sides of the base in thick card. The height of the sides has been planned in the box design.

MEASURING LENGTH OF SIDES The length of the short sides is measured by laying the covered base of the box onto the sheet of thick card and marking the width of the base. This is much quicker and more accurate than measuring with a ruler. But do make sure that a set square is used to make the corners an accurate 90° before cutting the card.

The length of the long sides is equal to the length of the covered base plus two thicknesses of the thick card. Use two pieces of off-cut card to place beside the covered base to measure this length. This allows for the long side to butt over the ends of the short sides (Fig. 26), which gives a good strong corner with a neat finish. It is impossible to get a good corner if all the side pieces are cut to the same measurements as the sides of the base without an overlap.

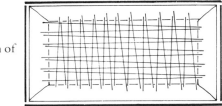

Fig. 26. Measuring for the length of the sides

If a flush-sided box is being made, the lip of the lid can be cut at the same time as the base sides. This will ensure that they are exactly the same length. The depth of the lip will have been determined in the design.

PADDING SIDES If the box requires padding on the outside, with anything from a piece of felt to quite heavy wadding, it now has to be lightly glued onto the side pieces of card, which have had their cut edges sandpapered smooth. The padding has to be trimmed to the same size as the card.

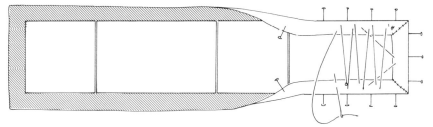

Fig. 27. Sides laid and pinned on the fabric, with the end corners mitred and the lacing started

COVERING SIDES Cut the fabric for the sides (see JOINS IN SIDES, p. 27). Having determined the position of the join or joins in the fabric, the material needed is the total length of the pieces of card in each section plus 1½in (4 cm) all round for turnings.

Lay the padded side of the first long side onto the wrong side of the fabric, pin into position on the straight grain, mitre the two corners at one end and begin lacing the material across the width (Fig. 27). A couple of lacing stitches will be needed to keep the turning between the mitred corners taut. Having laced the length of the first piece of card, push a short side of cut card tight against the first long piece. Pin into position and resume lacing. Continue in this way until all the sides required are tightly laced into position, then mitre the last two corners. If the first pair of corners were not mitred at the start, it will be found that, as the second and third pieces of card are pushed into position, the original piece has been displaced and there is no longer a turning to mitre and cover the end. It is also likely that the padding will have become wrinkled up with the movement, and a new start will have to be made. If, because of a shortage of fabric or because of the design of the material, there is to be a join on each corner, then each piece of card is laced separately, as for the base (Fig. 10, page 24).

Pin the side join or joins into position, making sure that all the corners lie correctly; that is, the short sides inside the long sides (Fig. 26). By having the short sides inside the long sides, a clean unbroken appearance is given to the front of the box.

Joining Side Seam or Seams

Ladder-stitch is used for all the main seams of the box (see GENERAL CONSTRUCTION, page 25, Figs 12 and 13). A lot of boxes have a weakness at the top edge of their corner joins, where there is bound to be wear and tear. If the ladder-stitch is started 1 in (3 cm) below the top edge and worked up to that top corner, adjusting the side pieces to get them absolutely level, it is then possible to sew down the full height of the side to the base edge. The first piece of double stitching will help enormously to keep the sides firm (Fig. 28).

Fig. 28. Joining a corner. Direction of stitching to give a double row at the top edge to take any strain

Sewing Base to Sides

Push the completed sides over the base and pin into position. If they do not fit, the chances are that the short sides are not lying correctly within the long sides and completely different measurements are made. They are easily 'clicked' into their correct positions. If the joins have been sewn up with the sides in the incorrect positions, then unfortunately they have to be unpicked, repositioned and sewn up again.

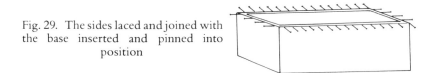

Fig. 29. The sides laced and joined with the base inserted and pinned into position

Having pinned the sides onto the base (Fig. 29), ladder-stitch together. If the 3 in (7 cm) ahead of where one is stitching is unpinned as you sew, it is possible to push the base up a fraction to make it easier to get the needle through the fabric edge and to push the base down a fraction to let the needle pass through the fabric on the edge of the sides. Otherwise a curved needle is most helpful.

Square Box

The construction of a square box is exactly the same as for a rectangular box, but care has to be taken with the making up of the strip that forms the sides of the box because, although the outside measurements of the sides of a square box are all equal, the sides still have a pair of long sides that butt over the ends of a pair of short sides (Fig. 26). The short pair equal the measurement of one side of the square base, while the long pair are the same measurement, plus two thicknesses of the card being used. This enables the sides to butt onto each other in the usual way. It is only too easy to lace them into the fabric in the wrong order, so it is advisable to mark each piece of card as it is cut for the sides either 'long' or 'short', as it is difficult to tell at a glance which is which.

Naturally, the same care has to be taken in making up the lip of a lid.

Lining

Thin card is normally used for the lining. The base piece is made up first and then dropped into position. The sides, in one long strip or four independent pieces sewn together are placed on top of the base lining, so keeping it in position. The lining sides only have to be sewn to the lining base if fittings are going to be constructed.

BASE LINING Measure the inside of the box for the base lining and cut out in thin card. Allow space for the thickness of the lining when it is turned over the edge of the card for lacing. If velvet is to be used, it takes up quite a lot of room.

Wadding can either be stuck onto the base card or the fabric can be quilted. If quilting is used, do cut away the wadding from the turnings to avoid bulkiness taking up space in the box.

The lining is pinned and laced into position over the card just like the original base (Fig. 10, page 24). Place in position before measuring for the side pieces.

SIDE LININGS The measurements for the lining sides are the same principle as for the main sides of the box, that is, the short sides sit inside and butt onto the long sides. The length of the long sides is the internal measurement of the length of the box. The short sides are the internal measurements of the width of the box, minus two thicknesses of the card being used. Due to the varying thicknesses of the padding and fabric which must be allowed for, it is necessary to cut the card and pin the lining round it, with its padding, to check that it all fits. If the card is too long, it forces the box out of shape and the lining bows in the middle. If it is too short, there are unsightly gaps.

The height of the side linings is dependent on the type of lid being used. The choice of lid also influences the weight of card required (page 47).

Do not measure the height of any side lining until the base lining is completed and in position, as it takes up a lot of room and needs to be taken into account.

SIDE LINING TO BE USED WITH AN OVERLAPPING LID (Fig. 32, page 47) Thin card is used for the lining sides, and it should be level with the outside of the box when finally finished.

RISING LINING TO BE USED WITH A FLUSH LID (Fig. 41, page 51) The side lining holds the lid in position in this design, so as it is a part of the main construction, thick card is used for the side lining. The distance that it extends above the base is determined by the lip of the lid. The lining must be at least $\frac{1}{2}$ in (15 mm) less than the depth of the lip to allow plenty of clearance for the lining of the lid. If not, the padding in the lid lining can push the lid up on the side lining and there will be a gap between the lip and the base. The lining fabric will show and it will look very untidy.

SIDE LINING TO BE USED WITH A DROP-IN LID (Fig. 42, page 51) Here the lid sits inside the box, with the top of the lid level with the sides and resting on the lining. The side lining needs to be cut $\frac{1}{4}$ in (5 mm) less than the height of the base sides. The side linings can be of thin card, but thick card can also be used if preferred.

SIDE LINING TO BE USED WITH A POP-ON LID (Fig. 43, page 54) or HINGED LID (Fig. 44, page 54) These lids lie on top of the box sides and their linings extend down inside the box to keep them firmly in position. Thin card is used for the side linings and it needs to be cut level with the box sides.

Cut the card for the side linings, pad, cover and lace in the normal way for all designs except the rising lining in a flush-sided box.

RISING LINING FOR A FLUSH-SIDED BOX This does need to be handled slightly differently, as more turning is needed to cover where the lining is exposed on the outside of the box. Care must be taken that the lacing stitches do not show above the sides of the base (Fig. 30). For the same reason, normal mitred corners are not adequate and the fabric has to be folded and stitched in order to have a tidy finish on both sides (Fig. 31).

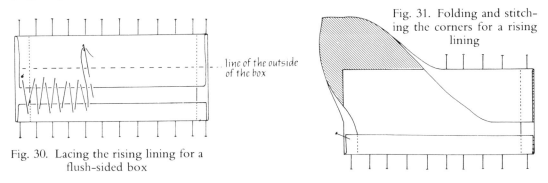

line of the outside of the box

Fig. 30. Lacing the rising lining for a flush-sided box

Fig. 31. Folding and stitching the corners for a rising lining

STITCHING LININGS TO BASE OF BOX When the lining sides have been completed, they are dropped into position to hold the base lining in place and the top edge is ladder-stitched to the base of the box.

Do not sew the lining to the base of the box if fittings are required, as they have to be completed first.

Various Types of Lid

Overlapping Lid (Fig. 32)
It is an unfortunate proportion if the lip of an overlapping lid breaks the side in half: it is a very much better proportion if it is only a third of the depth, leaving two thirds of the base visible. If a lip is required to come down to the base of the box, then it is essential to have a platform fixed to the base of the box, otherwise it is extremely difficult to remove the lid from the base (Fig. 33).

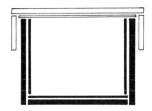

Fig. 32. Overlapping lid

Fig. 33. Overlapping lid on base platform

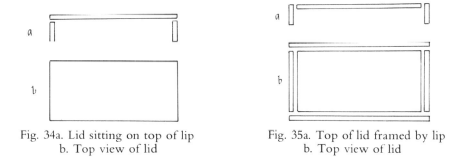

Fig. 34a. Lid sitting on top of lip
b. Top view of lid

Fig. 35a. Top of lid framed by lip
b. Top view of lid

For a lid with a lip, there are two ways for the top of the lid to be attached to its lip.

The first and normal way is for the top to sit on the lip (Fig. 34) giving a clean, seamless look to the top of the lid, with nothing to break the line of the embroidery.

There are cases, though, where it is an advantage to frame the top of the lid by the lip (Fig. 35). In the case of the Jewellery Box (Plate 10), the embroidery was backed by a silk organza, which would have worn very badly if it had been taken over the edge of the lid and regularly handled. Here it is set in and framed by the lip, so that wear is avoided.

9 Turquoise jewellery box showing velvet-lined tray with tabs for lifting. Lid and base lined with kingfisher blue rayon seamed in triangles

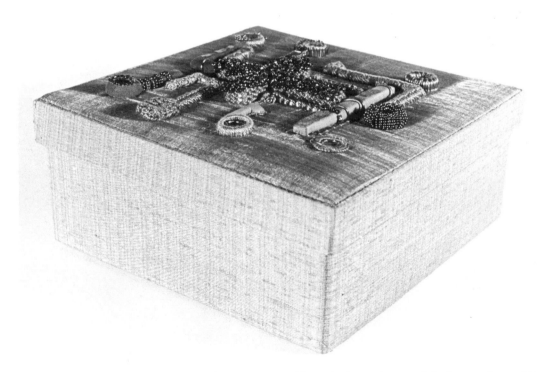

10 Turquoise jewellery box in slubbed rayon curtain fabric, with overlapping lid. $8\frac{5}{8}$ in $\times 8\frac{1}{2}$ in $\times 3\frac{1}{2}$ in (21 cm $\times$ 21 cm $\times$ 9 cm)

The other case is where two different fabrics are being incorporated in a box. An entire box of canvas-work can be very clumsy, but used with leather it is most successful. If the top of the lid is canvas-work, it is greatly enhanced by being framed by the lip covered in leather. This pulls it all together and helps the general design enormously.

First cut the lip of the lid in thick card. The height of the lip will have been decided on in the design. Please note that anything less than $\frac{3}{4}$ in (2 cm) is difficult to handle, and the card can crack under inexperienced fingers. The length of the card is measured in the usual way. Using the base of the box, mark the outside measurements of the short sides. The measurement for the long sides is the outside measurement of the base, plus two thicknesses of the thick card. The sides of the lip will then butt onto each other in the same way as the base.

PADDING A LIP OF A LID The outside of the lip is padded to match the base of the box. The inside of the lip is never padded, as it would only add bulk and could get disturbed by the continual movement of taking the lid on and off.

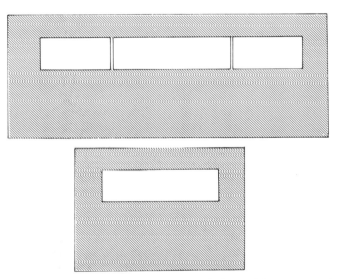

Fig. 36. Card laid on fabric with turnings for lip of lid which has joins on the two back corners of the long side

Fig. 37. Beginning to cover the lip of the lid

COVERING A LIP OF A LID The lip of a lid is covered with one piece of material, as it would be very bulky and cumbersome if it was lined with a second piece of covered card. Make the lip up with the same joins as the base, making sure that their positions match. Cut the fabric for each section which is the length of the total pieces of card in that section, plus turnings at both ends. The width is twice the depth of the lip, plus a minimum of 2 in (5 cm) for turnings (Fig. 36). Lay the first piece of card onto the fabric with 1-in (3-cm) turning along one edge and fold the turning along one end (Fig. 37). Fold over the rest of the fabric to enclose the card (Fig. 38) and pin into position. It is important to pull the turnings which lie along the length of the card round the edge to lie at 90° to the card (Fig. 39). These turnings will lie underneath the top of the lid and be hidden from view by the lining of the lid. Unless this seam is pulled round the corner, its stitching can show on the top edge of the lip, as the top of the lid fails to cover it.

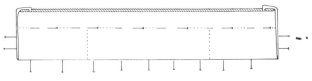

Fig. 38. Three pieces of the lip pinned into position for covering

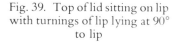

Fig. 39. Top of lid sitting on lip with turnings of lip lying at 90° to lip

Fig. 40. Turnings of lip pulled down to allow top of lid to sit on them and be framed by lip

If the top of the lid is being inset in the lip, and being framed by the lip (Fig. 35, page 47), the seam needs to be pulled down to a $\frac{1}{4}$ in (5 mm) below the top of the lip to allow the lid to rest on it (Fig. 40).

Back-stitch the seam with matching thread and ladder-stitch the folded ends. Make sure that the folded ends lie on the inside of the lip with the seam, otherwise they can break the smooth finish of the outside of the lip. Now make up the lip into shape by ladder-stitching the join or joins, with the same method as the base sides. Check that the short sides are lying correctly inside the long sides.

MEASURING FOR TOP OF LID WITH LIP (Fig. 34, page 47) Place the lip of the lid in position over the base of the box. Pin the turnings of the lip into mitres at the corners and trim off the surplus material. Turn the box upside down onto thick card and mark the position of the outside edges of the lip. Using a set square, draw out the shape for the top of the lid. Cut out and sandpaper the card. Lay the cut card on the box with the lip still in its proper position and check it for size. If the sides seem to sit correctly level with the lip but the actual corners jut out rather sharply, it is perfectly in order to rub the corner points off with fine sandpaper.

MEASURING FOR TOP OF LID FRAMED BY LIP (Fig. 35, page 47) Measure from the inside of the lip across the box to inside the lip on the opposite side. Repeat this in the other direction. Remember to allow a little space for the fabric, which will be laced over the edge. Draw out the measurements on thick card, using a set square. Cut out the card and sandpaper.

MAKING UP TOP OF LID Pad as required and pin the fabric over the card, watching that any embroidery is correctly placed with the grain parallel to the edge of the card.

Lace the fabric over the card in the usual way. It is now ready to ladder-stitch to the lip. Pin into position and stitch.

Line the lid by cutting thin card to size, allowing space for the turnings of the lining. Either pad the card or quilt the lining as required. Pin and lace the lining.

Before fixing the lining into the lid, first apply a little glue to the underside of the turnings from the lip and press them firmly onto the lid. This helps to keep everything flat. Put a little glue onto the central area of the underside of the lid and drop the lining down onto it. The lid lining will still need a stitch or two to hold it, and even with a curved needle, this is not very easy. A couple of stitches at each corner is sufficient and these can be knotted off and the ends pushed under the lining, so that nothing shows.

Flush Lid with a Rising Lining (Fig. 41 and Plate 7, page 37)
This is a neat and practical shape. The lining juts up above the sides of the base of the box and holds the lip of the lid in position. It is extremely useful if a tray is required in the box, as it gives the maximum interior depth to hold the tray, without looking heavy.

The measurements for this lip are the same as for the sides of the base and should have been cut out at the same time for complete accuracy. The method for making up the lip and the choice of having the top of the lid lying on top of the lip, or framed by it, is exactly the same as for the overlapping lid.

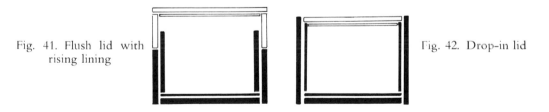

Fig. 41. Flush lid with rising lining

Fig. 42. Drop-in lid

Drop-in Lid (Fig. 42)
This is the simplest construction where the lid sits within the sides of the box and rests on the lining, which is $\frac{1}{4}$ in (5 mm) below the top edge of the box.

The drop-in lid is the same size as the base of the box and should have been cut out at that stage. This piece of thick card is padded, covered and laced in the usual way. Care must be taken to mitre and sew off the corners tidily, as a band of the turning will show round the edge on the underside of the lid.

11 Hexagon patchwork box with a drop-in lid. 10 in × 6 in × 2½ in (25 cm × 15 cm × 6 cm)

12 Octagon box with gold-work lion's head. 5 in × 4½ in × 2½ in (13 cm × 12 cm × 6 cm).
Belinda Montagu

As a drop-in lid is sunk into the box, it is necessary to have some sort of method of lifting the lid. A tag can be fitted between the lid and the lining, or various types of handles fixed to the lid, right through the card before the lining is stitched into position (Plate 12).

The lining is made of thin card and is cut so that it will sit inside the side lining of the base. Pad and lace this piece and then ladder-stitch it into position on the underside of the lid.

Pop-on Lid (Fig. 43 and Plate 13)
This lid lies on top of the sides of the box and is prevented from slipping out of position by a thick lining to the lid, which protrudes down inside the box and holds the lid firm.

13 Leaf-shaped box with gold-work decoration open to show the two pop-on lids. 9 in × 6 in × 2½ in (23 cm × 15 cm × 6 cm). *Beryl Morgan*

It is cut in thick card, either to be flush with the sides of the base, or to extend to give a finger-hold for lifting. How far it extends beyond the sides of the base depends on the design, but it is necessary to guard against it looking top heavy.

It is padded, covered and laced with fabric in the usual way. Care is needed to ensure that sufficient turnings are left to give a neat band on the underside edge. It is not easy to make the mitres tidy enough, as the border up to the lid lining can be quite wide on this type of lid. Embroidered motifs or pieces of braid on the corners can be very helpful to cover up a difficult construction point. It is important that any addition of this kind is an integral part of the design.

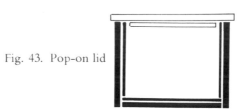

Fig. 43. Pop-on lid

The lid lining is in thick card and is cut to sit firmly inside the box and so hold the lid in position. It is padded, covered and laced in the normal way and then ladder-stitched into position, making sure that it is centrally placed.

Hinged Lid (Fig. 44 and Plate 4, page 32)
This lid sits on top of the sides of the box and is hinged with a strip of fabric to the base along one side.

It is cut in thick card and can either be flush with the base sides, or extend beyond them, according to the design. The lid needs to be padded, covered and laced in preparation for attaching the hinge. The same care needs to be taken over the underside turnings as for the pop-on lid.

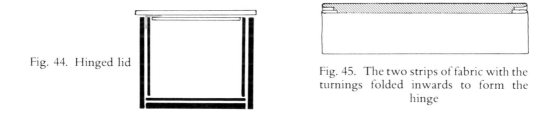

Fig. 44. Hinged lid

Fig. 45. The two strips of fabric with the turnings folded inwards to form the hinge

The lid lining of thin card is cut to lie inside the base of the box to help hold the lid firm. The hinge obviously does a great deal towards this, which is why a lid lining of thick card is unnecessary. The lining card can now be padded and covered.

Prepare the hinge by making 3-in (7-cm) wide strips of the fabric used for the outside of the box and the lining, the length being the internal measurement of the side of the box where the hinge will be fixed, plus turnings at each end. Fold in the turnings and lay the two strips together with the raw edges inside (Fig. 45). Ladder-stitch the ends together. Should the fabrics have any give in them and be likely to stretch, they should be interlined with a piece of calico of the same width and the exact length of the prepared strip, no turnings being necessary.

Fold the hinge in half lengthways, and place this fold to the line on the lid where the hinge is required, with the raw edges towards the outside. This could be on the actual edge of the lid (Fig. 46), but if the lid extends beyond the sides of the box, the hinge will be set in from the edge of the lid by the width of the overhang (Fig. 47). Pin into position and oversew with matching thread. Pull half the hinge down onto the wrong side of the box and herringbone onto the turnings of the laced lid (Fig. 48).

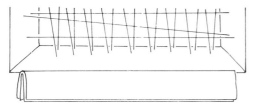

Fig. 46. The hinge folded in half and placed on the edge of the lid ready for stitching

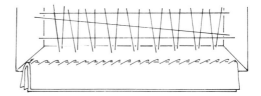

Fig. 47. The hinge set in from the edge of lid as an alternative position, and the first line of stitching completed

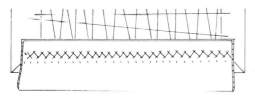

Fig. 48. The hinge sewn onto the lid

Fig. 49. The lid pinned into position

Fig. 51. A folded strip of fabric to make a stay

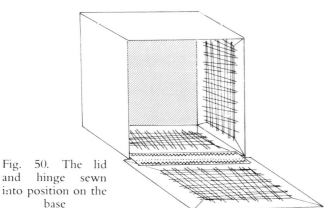

Fig. 50. The lid and hinge sewn into position on the base

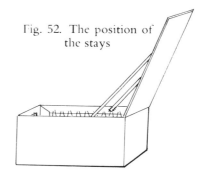

Fig. 52. The position of the stays

The second half of the hinge can now be fixed to the base of the box. Lay the lid on top of the base and pin the hinge into its correct position from the outside (Fig. 49). Open the lid and sew the hinge tightly in position on the laced turnings of the base with two rows of herringbone (Fig. 50).

The stays to stop the lid falling back can be made of various materials. Fine chain, cord or a fold of fabric (Fig. 51) are a few suggestions. The positioning of the stays is one third from the back of the box on the base and one third from the front on the lid (Fig. 52). Sew the stays into position on the turnings of the base and the turnings of the lid.

Fig. 53. Tab attached between the top of the lid and the lid lining

The base lining can then be put in and sewn to the base along its top edge. Next the lining of the lid can be pinned into position and ladder-stitched with a curved needle.

If a small tab is needed for lifting the lid, this should be sewn to the turnings of the lid at the centre front and its raw edges concealed by the lid lining (Fig. 53).

Oval and Round Boxes

Plan the size, proportions and type of lid for the box. Choose the material suitable for its purpose and design the embroidered areas (Plate 14).

14 Oval box in coral dupion curtain fabric with raised and padded gold, silk and bead work. Open to show organdie shadow-work lining. 11½ in × 8 in × 4 in (29 cm × 20 cm × 10 cm). *Mollie Collins*

Cutting Base for Round Box

Using a compass and a very sharp, hard pencil, draw out a circle on thick card. Cut it out with the Stanley knife, remembering only to 'draw' with it the first time round, then press more heavily on the second circuit and the blade will remain in the 'tramline' and cut a clean edge.

Cutting Base for Oval and Similar Shaped Boxes

A pie-dish or oval plate can often give the required shape, and can be drawn and cut round. If nothing of a suitable size is available, oval and related shapes can be constructed (Figs 54, 55, 56).

If a drop-in lid is needed, cut another piece of heavy card exactly the same size as the base at the same time.

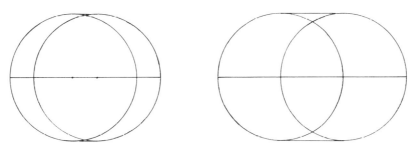

Fig. 54 and Fig. 55. Constructing an oval

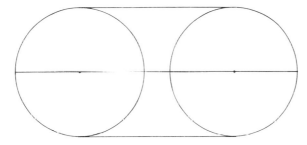

Fig. 56. Constructing a D ended shape

PADDING BASE Having smoothed off the card with sandpaper, lightly glue a thin padding of felt or similar weight of fabric to the base. If a thick fabric like tweed or leather is being used for the outside of the box, this will be unnecessary.

COVERING BASE Lay the felted side of the base onto the wrong side of the fabric and allow 1½ in (4 cm) of turning all round. Pin the fabric onto the card, making sure that the straight grain lies on the diameter of the circle, or through the middle of the shape.

The easiest way to lace fabric over any curved or unusual shaped piece of card is to run a gathering thread round the shape first, ½ in (15 mm) from the raw edge (Fig. 57). Draw this up and then lace across the shape (Fig. 58).

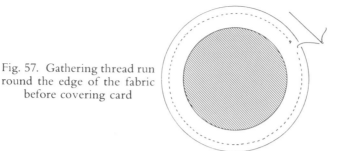

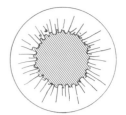

Fig. 57. Gathering thread run round the edge of the fabric before covering card

Fig. 58. The fabric pulled up ready for lacing over the card

The Sides of Round, Oval and all Curved Shaped Boxes
There are three basic methods of forming the sides of these boxes:

1. THIN CARD The thin card is wrapped round the base and overlapped to form two layers of card.
2. THICK CARD The thick card is dampened with a foam rubber sponge or steamed and moulded to shape round the base.
3. CARDBOARD TUBES For round boxes only (Plate 6, page 35). The thick card rolls which are used by stores for rolling carpet round can be cut to the required height and form very strong sides for round boxes.

   The disadvantages of this method are that the size of the box is restricted to whatever size tubes are available and, secondly, that the base has to be cut to fit the tube, rather than the side made to fit the base.

CUTTING SIDE IN THIN CARD Cut a long strip of thin card, the width being the desired height of the box.

Using the covered base of the box, wrap the card round the base, using clips or pegs to hold the card together where it overlaps.

If a small box is being made, the card need only be long enough to wrap round to form two layers. Make sure that the card overlaps the join by at least 2 in (5 cm) (Fig. 59). If a larger box is being constructed, each layer of card needs to be cut separately, as the sheet of card may not be long enough to extend round the base more than once.

Fig. 59. Thin card wrapped round the base to form two layers

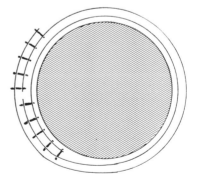

Fig. 60. Two separate layers of thin card wrapped round the base

Wrap the first layer of card round the base and overlap by at least 2 in (5 cm), then clip to maintain correct size. Trim off any surplus card and sew the join off with crochet cotton and a large stitch. Take the second strip of card of equal measurements and butt the end of it to the cut edge of the first layer. Clip into position and continue wrapping the second layer of card round the first, clipping as you go, to prevent air spaces between the layers of card. Lap over the original join by at least 2 in (5 cm) and stitch into position (Fig. 60). The two layers can either be stitched together with a thick needle, as there are actually three thicknesses of card, or the second layer can be slipped off, stitched and then re-positioned. A piece of Scotch-tape should be laid over the cut edge to obviate any bump on the card.

It is possible to join the strips of card first by overlapping the two or more pieces to the required length, and stitching in turn, and then to use as one long strip. Wrap around the covered base continuously to form two layers, overlap as before and stitch into position. It really depends on the size of the box being made and the length of card available as to which method will be most efficient. Three layers of card might be needed on a 16-in (40-cm) box.

When wrapping the card round the covered base, remember to allow space for the turnings of the material which will be covering the sides of the box. If a thin silk or cotton is being used, the space is negligible, but leather, tweed, velvet and textured fabrics need to have an allowance left for them. Before wrapping the card round the covered base, lay a piece of the selected fabric over the base and then wrap the card round.

CUTTING SIDE IN THICK CARD Cut a strip of thick card a little longer than the circumference of the covered base, with the width equal to the required height of the side of the box. Chamfer one narrow end (Fig. 61). Whatever the size of the box, the strip should be cut from the length of the sheet of card, as this will mould more easily than from across the width.

Fig. 61. The thickness of the card being cut at an angle to chamfer it

Fig. 62. Two chamfered ends ready for joining

Dampen the card with a wet foam sponge or a steaming kettle, to make the card pliable. Do not dampen the second end of the strip of card at this stage, as it will need to be trimmed off accurately and the end chamfered to fit the first end (Fig. 62). Be careful not to over-soak it, but if it is not wet enough the card will crack.

The card must be wrapped around the base to ascertain the exact length required, as it is more than the flat measurement indicates. The thickness of the card going round the curves requires more length than is realized. Bend the damp strip of card carefully round the covered base. As it is moulded into position, pin into place through the strip into the edge of the base card, until it is possible to determine where the second end should be cut to size and chamfered. Pin the join into position and tie tapes round the side to hold the join in position (Fig. 63). Leave to dry off, which can take twenty-four hours if not placed in a warm area. When it is completely dry, put some glue onto the chamfered edges and Scotch-tape into position. The Scotch-tape can remain there permanently as extra support (frontispiece).

If a lid with a rising lining is being made (page 51), the lip should be cut at this stage, using the same method as that used for the base sides. This makes sure that they are both of exactly the same size.

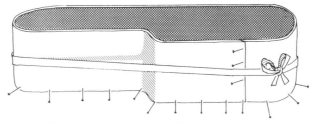

Fig. 63. Thick card moulded round the base, pinned and tied with tape so that it can dry in shape

PADDING THE SIDE The amount of padding required depends on the box design. Glue is spread thinly over the outside of the sides and felt or wadding moulded round it, with the join placed at the centre back and meeting edge to edge, not overlapping, which would cause a lump. The top and bottom edges can be trimmed so that the padding is level with the edges. Allow to dry.

COVERING SIDES To achieve a really good finish on a curved surface, a fabric with a certain amount of stretch is necessary. Leather gives beautiful results, so do the new stretchy panné velvets and good quality jerseys of all types. Otherwise, the fabric must be cut on the cross, to avoid wrinkling on the top and bottom edges of the side. The join needs to be placed on the centre back of the box side and always made on the straight grain (Figs. 64, 65).

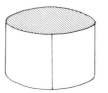

Fig. 64. Fabric for sides cut on the straight grain and showing position of the seam

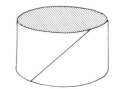

Fig. 65. Fabric for sides cut on the cross and showing the position of the seam

Cut out the fabric with 1½-in (4-cm) turnings all round, or more if the fabric is likely to fray badly. Fold in the turning on one short end and place for the centre back join, pin into position (Fig. 66). Begin pulling the fabric round the side, pulling it tight both lengthways and widthways (Fig. 67). Start to lace on the inside. Continue stretching the fabric round, pinning and lacing until the centre back is reached, trim off any surplus, leaving ⅜ in (10 mm) to be turned under. Allow the folds of the seam to lie ⅛ in (3 mm) apart. Stitch up the seam with ladder-stitch, making sure to sew right over onto the inside where the lacing lies. As the ladder-stitch is worked, pull the seam together, so keeping up a good firm tension on the fabric (Fig. 68).

The side is now ready to place over the base, pin and ladder-stitch together.

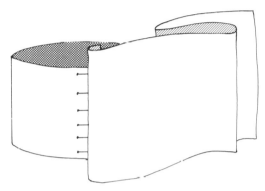

Fig. 66. Placing the fabric for a centre back join

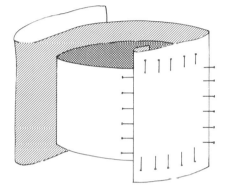

Fig. 67. Pulling the fabric tight round the sides, pinning into position before lacing

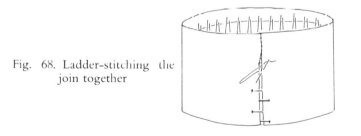

Fig. 68. Ladder-stitching the join together

Lining Base and Side

The lining is made from thin card. As for rectangular boxes, the base lining is cut to shape, padded and covered, then dropped into position before any measurements are taken for the side lining.

The side lining is made from one strip of thin card wrapped round the inside of the box to the required size. Allow a 2-in (5-cm) overlap of card as before and stitch together.

For the rising lining of a flush-sided lid, a heavier lining is required, as in the rectangular boxes, so use two layers of thin card.

The height of the lining is dependent on the type of lid being made and is exactly the same principle as for rectangular boxes (page 46).

PADDING SIDE LINING The sides are padded as required in the usual manner (page 45), with the padding butting at the join.

COVERING SIDE LINING A bias strip gives the best results and is easiest with a fabric that has some give, rather than a stiff lining fabric. As on the outside of a curved box, the join must be on the straight grain and is best positioned on the centre front of the box, as it will show less there. Fold in the turning and pin the first seam edge into position, similar to the covering of the outside of curved sides. Stretch the fabric and pin into position, beginning the lacing on the outside of the card. Continue stretching, pinning and lacing until the lining is completely covered. Join the seam, using the same method as for the outside.

The side lining only needs to be sewn to the base lining if fittings are being made, otherwise the sides keep the base in position.

The top edge of the side lining can now be ladder-stitched to the sides of the box if there are to be no fittings.

Overlapping Lip

The depth of the overlapping lip will depend on the box design. It is cut from a strip of thin card and wrapped round the covered sides in the same method as the sides of the box made from thin card.

As for the sides of the base, it is necessary to allow space for the thicker fabrics like leather, velvet, tweed and those fabrics with a heavy texture. A layer of the fabric should be placed round the base sides before placing the card for the lip round it. This will ensure an exact fit of the lip.

Two layers of card are required to give the necessary strength. Three layers are needed for a 16-in (40-cm) box.

If a lip is being made from thick card, it is moulded round the side of the base using the same method as for the base side. Before beginning, slip the covered base into a thin plastic bag and press out the air. This will prevent the base from being marked by the wet card being used for the lip.

PADDING LIP The lip of the lid must have the same weight of padding as the side of the base of the box.

Fig. 69. Stitching the seam on the lip of the lid

COVERING LIP The method of covering the lip is the same as for rectangular boxes (page 50). If a bias strip is used for covering the base side, then a bias strip must be used for covering the lip. Ladder-stitch the seam together when the fabric has been stitched over the card (Fig. 69), making sure that the seam lines up with the seam on the base side of the box when the top of the lid is positioned on the lip.

MEASURING FOR TOP OF LID WITH A LIP For a circular lid, if a lip is being used, place the lip on the base side, and measure across the top where the lid is required in two directions, at right angles to each other. This is in case the shape has been slightly distorted in the construction. If one measurement is 6 in (15 cm) and the other 7 in (17 cm), then the diameter of the lid will be 6½ in (16 cm) and the radius of the circle to be drawn will be 3¼ in (8 cm).

For an unusual curved shape, place the lip on the base, turn the box upside down and draw round the lip with a pencil onto thick card.

For a box with no lip, draw round the base to get the exact size, then a measurement can be added or subtracted all the way round the shape to allow the lid to extend beyond the sides of the box, or be small enough to drop in and rest on the side lining, whichever is required.

The basic design principles, weight of card and general approach are exactly the same as for the lids of rectangular boxes (pages 51–54).

Cut in thick card, pad, cover and lace the shape. Attach any necessary knob or tab and line with covered card.

Fittings

When planning the fittings, be careful to leave enough space within each section to be of use, as it is very easy to put too much into a small area.

Watch that the fittings are of equal height, unless there is a specific reason, so that the interior has a neat, planned appearance. The walls of the compartments must never rise above the top edge of the bottom half of the box, otherwise the lid will not fit.

Divisions

The inside of the box can be divided up to meet the requirements of its use.

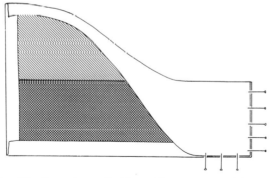

Fig. 70. Covering a divider with one piece of fabric

The dividing walls are best cut from thick card, padded, then covered with one piece of fabric (Fig. 70). They can also be made by lacing two pieces of card separately, then placing them with the wrong sides together and ladder-stitching round the edge. With this method thin card can be used as the two layers should give enough strength, except for larger boxes. The disadvantage is that there is a seam on the top edge of the divider, which does not appear when covering a single piece of card by the previous method. However, if a different coloured fabric is required on each side of the partition, then this is the method to choose.

Care must be taken not to cut the dividers too long, as they can distort the shape of the box.

If the box is being partitioned into four compartments, a very neat way of cutting the dividers is to score the card at the junction of the walls and, bending the card at 90°, the pieces will lock together (Fig. 71). The wadding needs to be cut through on the score line to allow the pieces to fit together, otherwise they are covered separately as before (Fig. 70).

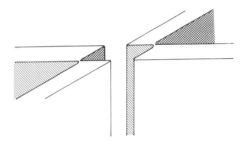

Fig. 71. Thick card scored so that dividers will lock together

The dividers are sewn to the lining of the box to hold them secure. To do this, the side lining and base lining are removed from the box and sewn together by whipping on the wrong side. The dividers are then pinned into position and long stitches are taken through the lining card and fabric and the needle slid down the edge of the covered dividers, then taken back through the lining and lining card. This is continued right round the edge of the divider.

Covered Compartments

If the divided sections are to be taken one stage further and turned into covered compartments, then it is necessary to line each compartment with fabric covered card, so that a drop-in lid made in the normal way (page 51) can be supported.

Ring Supports

The first type is made by sewing two padded thick card dividers together, leaving the top edge open to slot the rings into (Plate 15). Care must be taken not to have the ring support too high, otherwise there is not room for the large modern rings to sit without forcing the box lid out of position.

Another type can be made by padding and covering a wooden dowel rod, onto which the rings can be slid. This can be loose, resting into slots on the dividers, or on special supports attached to the side lining. If preferred, it can have a fabric hinge onto the lining and press stud into position on the opposite side.

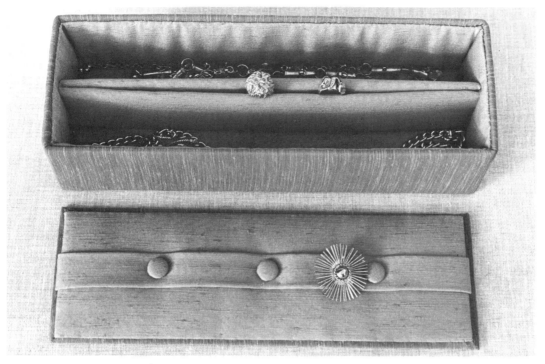

15 Fittings for a ring box. 12 in × 4 in × 3 in (30 cm × 10 cm × 7 cm)

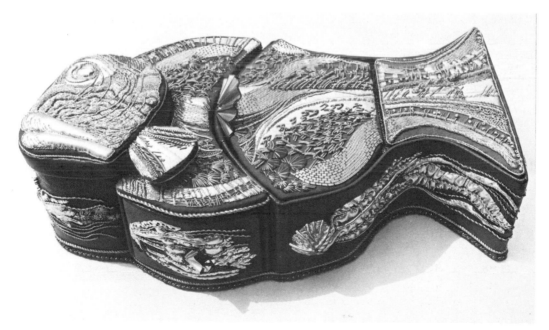

16 Fish jewellery box in gold-work on red leather. 12 in × 6 in × 3 in (30 cm × 15 cm × 8 cm).
Audrey Chorley

Ring trees can be made by covering lengths of pipe cleaner with gloving leather, the ends of which are passed down a short plastic tube to hold them neatly and securely together. This in turn is covered with matching leather and the whole is sewn to the base lining, so that it stands straight and firm (Plate 17).

17 Showing the overlapping lid making the fish's head, with a ring tree in that compartment, two side drawers, a hinged lid and a drop-in lid for the tail. *Audrey Chorley*

Trays (Plate 9, page 48)
If a tray is to be made for the box, the normal lining should only be padded with felt, as otherwise the lifting in and out of the tray will push the wadding out of position, apart from taking up too much space in the box.

The tray supports are made first out of thick card, cut in the usual manner, with the short sides sitting inside the long sides (Fig. 72). The card can be padded with wadding to give a richer area below the tray. The supports are laced with lining fabric, pushed into position and ladder-stitched along their top edge to the lining sides.

The tray sides and base are all cut in thick card, with a thin card lining on the base of the tray. The sides are measured, cut a fraction smaller than the tray supports, and covered as for a lip. The base of the tray will then be fitted into the sides. It has to be done in this order to ensure that the tray is a good fit.

Fig. 72a. Showing the position of the
tray supports

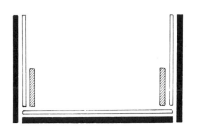

Fig. 72b. Showing the position of the tray supports within the lining of the base of the box

Fig. 73. Fabric folded to make tray handles

The tray sides are padded on the inside only and covered by the same method as the
lip of a lid (Figs. 38–40, page 50). The seam needs to be pulled well round (Fig. 40, page
50), to give space for the covered base of the tray to be accommodated.

A long strip of lining fabric is cut, folded and inserted, to make lifting tabs for the
tray (Fig. 73 and Fig. 25, page 41).

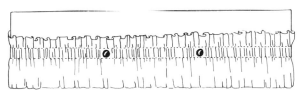

Fig. 74. A fold of fabric making the pocket, with elastic run through
to keep it taut

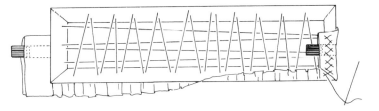

Fig. 75. Turnings of the pocket being wrapped round the side lining
and sewn into position

Workbox Fittings
Pockets on the lining sides are neater if they are made with inserted elastic to give more
space and to keep them tidy (Fig. 74).

Each piece of the side lining is laced separately. The pockets are then laid onto the
right side of each piece, pinned into position and the pocket turnings wrapped round

to the wrong side and herringboned to the turnings of the lining (Fig.75). The pocket can be caught back to the lining at intervals along each side. This can either be done by split-pin studs being taken right through the pocket, lining and card, or by neat stitching. If it is done by stitching, place a piece of tape or calico against the wrong side of the card to sew through, so that the stitching does not tear the lining card.

Elasticated strips of fabric can also be attached to the lid lining to take sewing tools. The ends of these are taken round to the wrong side of the lining and attached in the same way as the pockets (Fig. 76).

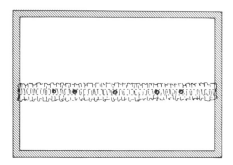

Fig. 76. Elasticated strip attached to the lid lining to take sewing tools

Boxes of Other than Four Sides

The method and order of construction is exactly the same as for a rectangular box, with the exception of the method for measuring the lengths of the sides.

As the sides of these boxes have corners with angles of more than 90°, the card has to be chamfered off to make each side butt onto the next.

Hexagonal Box
When cutting the sides, the measurement is the length of the side on the covered base plus one thickness of card, half a thickness being needed each end of the card to chamfer and butt onto the next side (Fig. 77).

Fig. 77. Construct a hexagon by marking the circumference of a circle with the radius. These six points joined up give the hexagon. The diagonals of the hexagon give the angle to chamfer the card for the sides

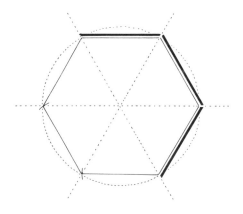

With any of these multi-sided boxes, it is advisable to Scotch-tape all the sides together and to place them round the covered base to ensure that they will fit. Do remember to allow enough ease in the fit for the turnings of the fabric which will be covering the sides.

The padding should be cut in one long strip to strengthen the corners. When glueing the sides onto it, place the pieces of card hard up against each other, leaving no gaps, having removed the Scotch-tape first. If material allows, use one long strip to cover all the sides at once.

FITTINGS It can be a problem to make dividing walls from each inside corner meet neatly in the centre, as once there are more than four pieces, it can get rather bulky. A way to overcome this problem is to make a repeat shape of the box as a central compartment and then to link its outside corners to the corners of the base by dividers (Plate 18).

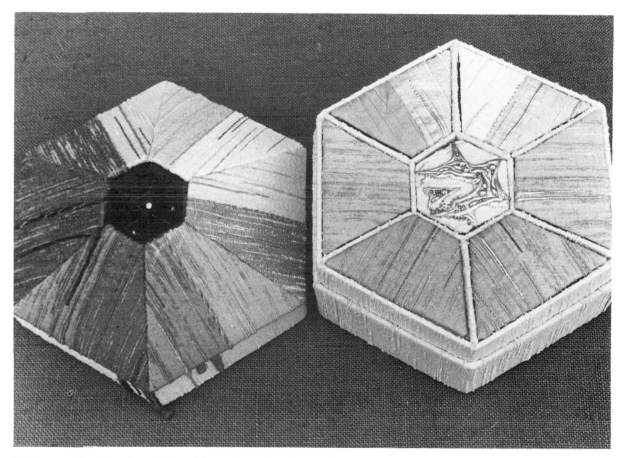

18 Twenty-four hour box in furnishing fabric. The domed lid is shaded grey to dark blue and depicts night. The inside is shaded creams and oranges and depicts day. The central compartment represents the sun and can be seen 'rising' through the dark hole in the lid. 10 in × 10 in × 4½ in (25 cm × 25 cm × 12 cm)

Writing-Paper Boxes

Designing

When designing these boxes it is essential to make sure that the compartments are of the right size to hold the required sheets of paper, envelopes, postcards, etc.

The traditional shape (Fig. 78) has the back in one piece with a flap lid and the front is lower than the back. This means that the top edges of the sides slope towards the front (Plates 19 and 20). This slope accommodates the necessary fittings, but there can be a variation of flaps and lids. In Fig. 79 a rounded flap attached to the back holds shut the two doors, which are hinged onto the sloping sides.

It is advisable to make a mock-up in card and to Scotch-tape it together to check that the proportions are pleasing and that the fittings are what is required. If enough space is allowed from front to back, a shallow tray for pens and pencils with a tiny box for stamps can be included.

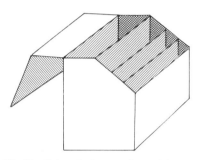

Fig. 78. Traditional shape of a writing-paper box

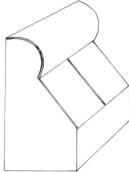

Fig. 79. Writing-paper case with rounded top

Fig. 80. Measuring the front and sides for a writing-paper box

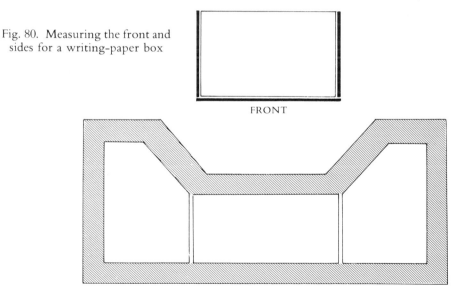

FRONT

Fig. 81. Front and sides of writing-paper box being covered with one piece of fabric

Base
Using thick card, the base is cut and covered in the usual way.

Sides and Front
The sides and front are cut next, with the sides butting onto the front. The front piece is the same as the length of the base, plus two thicknesses of card, as for a rectangular box, and the sides are the width of the base (Fig. 80). These three pieces of card are padded as required and then covered with one long piece of fabric (Fig. 81).

Back
The back is cut the length of the base plus two thicknesses of card, so that the sides butt onto it in the normal way. The height of the back must be equal to the height of the sides on the back edge.

19 Writing-paper box in brown kangaroo skin and black gloving suede, decorated with gold-work. 11 in × 6½ in × 8 in (28 cm × 16 cm × 20 cm). *Mollie Collins*

20 Writing-paper box opened to show black kid lining. *Mollie Collins*

Lid

The lid is cut in two sections of card to enable it to fold easily. Scoring the card does not work as well. These two pieces are made up as one with the back (Fig. 82). Use thick card for all three pieces. Glue them onto a calico or felt interlining, leaving a gap of $\frac{1}{8}$ in (3 mm) between the edges of the card to act as a hinge. Then pad as required and cover with one piece of fabric.

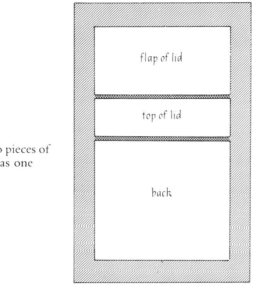

Fig. 82. Back with the two pieces of the lid being made up as one

flap of lid

top of lid

back

Lining

The lining is made in the normal way (page 45), sewing the partitions into position before dropping the whole lining into place. It can then be attached round the top edge of the box and round the edge of the flap lid.

Care needs to be taken not to get the lining of the lid too large, otherwise it slides forward and shows as the lid is shut. Adjusting the gap between the lining card in the hinge position should correct any problem that is found over this.

Boxes with Drawers

To obtain a really good fit on a chest of drawers it is necessary to work from the inside towards the outside; in other words the complete opposite to the method of construction previously used!

Drawers

The drawers are constructed first, using the same method as for a tray (see page 66). This means that the sides of the drawer are covered with one piece of fabric, so that no separate lining is needed for the sides. The base has a drop-in lining, which can be of a contrasting colour.

Handles

The handles of the drawers can be added when the drawers are completed, but this means that there is stitching showing on the inside of the drawer. A patch of material can be placed over this area, but a much better result is achieved by attaching the handle through the fabric and the card, before the fabric is backstitched round the card (Fig. 83). It is advisable to place a piece of calico next to the card on the inside to sew through. This prevents the thread cutting through the card as the handle is used.

The handles are an important part of the design (see the Islamic box, Colour plate A). These particular handles were made by scoring card (Fig. 84) and then covering with fabric and leather. Decoration was then added. Another idea for handle design is shown on Plate 21).

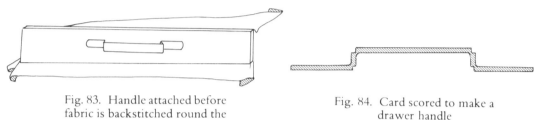

Fig. 83. Handle attached before fabric is backstitched round the card

Fig. 84. Card scored to make a drawer handle

21 Chest of drawers in Courtelle and leather. 15 in × 11¾ in × 11 in (37 cm × 30 cm × 28 cm). *Midge Burnett*

Make as many drawers as are required before starting on the casing. It is so much quicker and more accurate to cut all the pieces of card of the same length at the same time.

If two half drawers are required with a long drawer underneath, do remember that the half drawers are less than half the measurement of the long drawer, to allow space for the double thickness of card of the divider between them.

Drawer Casing

Each drawer has a casing like a matchbox cover. This covers the top, sides, base and back. It is made like an ordinary box, in thick card, but the fabric is on the inside and the lacing on the outside. It is neater if each piece of card is laced separately and then sewn together (Fig. 85). This drawer casing gives a neat interior to the whole box, when the drawers are removed.

It is very important to keep the lacing and mitred corners as flat as possible, so that the drawer casings stack neatly together. These now have to be ladder-stitched together right round on all sides, so that they form a rigid construction. A curved needle will be found very helpful for this.

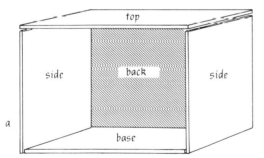

Fig. 85. Drawer casing

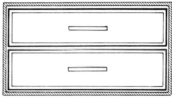

Fig. 86. Diagram to show the position of drawers, drawer casings and outside casing

Fig. 87. Position of the card for the outside casing

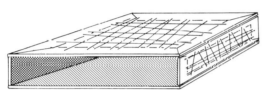

Outside Casing (Fig. 86)

It is now possible to measure and cut the card for the outside casing of the box. Cut the base first. This lies level with the drawer casing on the front edge. The sides are the depth of the base plus one thickness of card to allow for the back to be inset (Fig. 87b). In addition it is necessary to allow a fraction extra all round on the sides and back to give space for the turnings and lacing. This varies with the thickness of fabric, which is often bulkier than one expects. Fig. 87 shows the positioning of the card in making up the outside casing.

The sides and base can be covered in one piece of fabric. The back is laced separately and then inserted between the sides. The back is now stitched into place. The drawer casing is put inside and the front edges ladder-stitched to the front edges of the outside casing.

The card for the top is cut to extend to the outside edges of the casing, and this is then covered, laced and sewn into position.

Whilst fitting and pinning the casings together, it is helpful to put the drawers into position to keep everything as square and rigid as possible.

Thick card is used throughout, except the drop-in linings for the base of drawers.

Box with a drawer, or drawers, below
This is constructed in exactly the same way as the chest of drawers just described, but the sides and back are extended upwards to make the side and back walls of the box. A piece of card is then cut to make the front wall of the box, which has to lie between the sides. The box is then lined with thin card in the normal way and the required lid added, as in an ordinary box (Fig. 88).

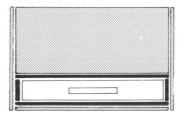

Fig. 88. Positioning of card for a box with a drawer underneath

Unusual Shaped Boxes and Those on a Base Platform

Base Platforms
Where the design indicates that the embroidery should flow down the sides of the box, it is often a help to have the lip of the lid taken down to the base of the box. This gives a larger area to work on and obliterates the problem of a break in the stitchery between the lip and the side of the box. When the lip is taken down to the base, it is essential to set the box on a platform to give an extended base, otherwise it is virtually impossible to remove the lid. The base platform, whilst giving the necessary leverage point to lift the lid, also adds a very pleasant addition to the design of the box (Plates 22 and 23). Naturally, a base platform can be used with any type of lid and any shape of box.

CONSTRUCTION OF BASE PLATFORM The base and sides of the box are made in the usual way and then, before the lining is inserted, the platform is made and attached into position.

First cut the thick card to the required shape and size. Stand the base of the box on it in order to check that the proportions are right. If a lid with a lip reaching down to the platform base is being used, allow for the thickness of the card, any padding and the fabric of the lip in estimating the width of the platform jutting out around the box.

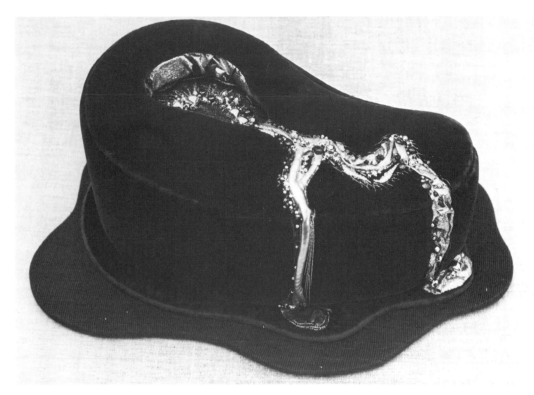

22 Purple velvet 'Drip' box with overlapping lid extending to a double base platform. 10½ in × 6¼ in × 4 in (27 cm × 16 cm × 10 cm)

23 Partition dividers in the 'Drip' box cut in one long strip with the side lining to control the waisted shape

Rub down the edges of the cut card with sandpaper and pad the upper side with felt. Next cover the upper side with fabric and lace into position on the underside.

It is impractical to cover the underside of the platform with fabric and lace on the upper side, allowing the turnings to cover the exposed area of the platform and the lacing to be concealed by the base of the box. The reason for this is that the thickness of the card does not allow perfect mitred corners to be worked on square or rectangular bases, likewise on any rounded edge where gathers would show, so that the upper side of the platform would be very untidy.

Having covered the platform on the upper side, the base of the box can be pinned into position. Three or four holes are now made through the base of the box and through the platform beneath, so that they can be sewn together with a linen thread or crochet cotton. A very heavy needle can make the holes; otherwise use an old stiletto. These three or four large stitches, knotted off tightly, are quite sufficient to hold the box and platform together. Using a curved needle, the base of the box should now be ladder-stitched to the platform where they meet.

The underside of the platform can now be covered with a matching coloured felt. Cut the felt to a shape to within $\frac{1}{4}$ in (5 mm) of the edge and hem into position. If it is now pressed with a steam iron, or an iron and damp cloth, the felt will shrink into place, leaving it beautifully flat and smooth.

Should the lacing on the underside of the platform be thick and bumpy, it is advisable to lay a thin layer of wadding over the lacing before applying the felt, so that the ridges of the lacing do not show through the felt and spoil the appearance.

If the design of the box demands it, then the platform can be made of more than one layer of card, either as a thicker block, or arranged as staggered steps.

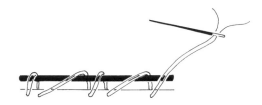

Fig. 89. Applying millinery wire to the edge of card

Unusual Shapes
The sides of curved shaped boxes, or parts of boxes, are sometimes difficult to keep in a controlled shape (Plates 24 and 25). This particularly applies to a fairly deep box of $3\frac{1}{2}$ or 4-in (9 or 10-cm) sides. The top edge of the sides can be inclined to pull away out of shape, especially when layers of thin card have been used in the construction. This happened to the box called 'the Drip' (Plate 22, page 77) and can occur with heart-shaped boxes. To prevent this happening, millinery wire is applied to the top edge of the card before it is padded and covered (Fig. 89). If the top edge is still inclined to pull out of shape, then it is necessary to plan the fittings so that they help to control the

24 Water-lily box. 7 in × 7 in × 5 in (18 cm × 18 cm × 13 cm) *Pamela Watts*

25 Water-lily box showing lid removed and wired petals

shape at the vulnerable points. The Drip box shows that this technique works very well. To keep the 'waist' of the box in position, the side linings and compartment dividers were cut in one long piece. Thin card was used, scored at the bends, then padded and laced with one long piece of fabric. Fig. 90 shows how it was placed to take the strain. If ordinary dividing walls were made there would have been too much strain on the stitching that held the dividers to the side linings and it would have been difficult to achieve a good finish.

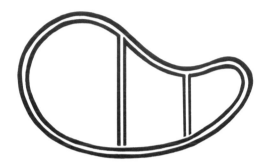

Fig. 90. Use of the lining and dividers to help control the shape of the box

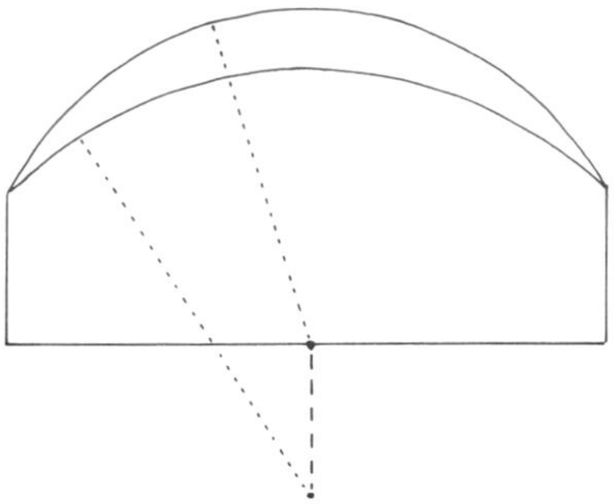

Fig. 91. Two alternative shapes constructed with a compass for the lid of a trunk box

Trunk Box (Plate 26)

The base of this box has a small rising lining to take the flush-type lid.

The lid is made of thick card. The sides of the lid are shaped as shown in Fig. 91. As shown in the diagram this shape can vary as required by the design, but it must have enough straight section before the start of the curve to take the rising lining of the base when the box is in the closed position. The sides of the lid are cut, sandpapered, padded with felt and laced with the fabric, leaving good-sized turnings.

Cut the thick card for the top of the lid. Allow a longer measurement than you think is required, as a piece of card cut to the same length as the curved edge of the side piece is not long enough. The thickness of the card makes it necessary to allow an extra $\frac{1}{4}$ in (5 mm) or so for the outside curve of the lid. It is much easier to cut it 1 in (3 cm) longer than necessary and then trim it off to the exact length when it has been curved into shape over the side pieces. As it is in thick card, it will need to be dampened, pinned and tied with tapes into position onto the sides. When it is dry, trim to the correct length, pad and lace with fabric. Ladder-stitch to the lid sides.

The lining of the lid has separate pieces for the sides and a long piece for the rounded top. The lining must lie well in from the edge of the lid to allow the rising lining to sit comfortably, otherwise the lid will not sit in a flush-sided position when the box is closed. This means that good turnings must be left when lacing the lid pieces.

This type of lid is usually made with a hinge inserted in the normal way (page 54).

The leather trimmings used in Plate 26 were all completed separately, then attached by a little glue and stitched into position using a curved needle when the construction of the box was completed.

26 Grey and silver chest, showing small rising lining to hold flush lid. Note two small leather hinges and chain stays. $8\frac{1}{4}$ in $\times$ $5\frac{1}{2}$ in $\times$ $6\frac{3}{4}$ in (21 cm $\times$ 14 cm $\times$ 17 cm)

Boxes in the Shape of Letters
Plate 27 shows a mock-up for the construction of the letter 'J'. A drop-in lid is the simplest and neatest for this type of construction.

The sides of the base are each cut to measurement, making sure that each piece butts onto the previous side to obtain strong corners. As long as they butt, it does not matter which piece butts onto which, as long as the sides can be covered with one long piece of fabric. Too many joins on the corners could be very cumbersome and spoil the entire box, so this design should not be attempted unless there is enough fabric to get a good result.

27 Mock-up of 'J' box in thick card to show sides butting onto each other and the drop-in lid. $7\frac{1}{2}$ in × 6 in × 2 in (19 cm × 15 cm × 5 cm)

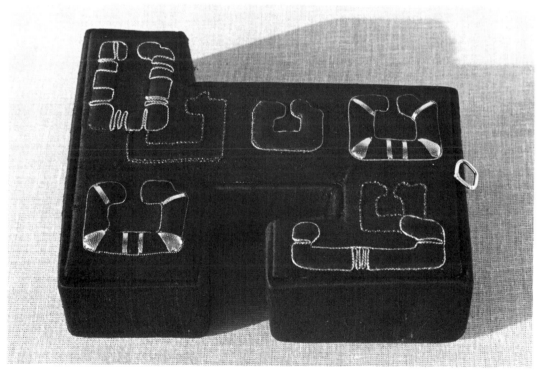

28 'J' box made up with leather and gold initials. $7\frac{1}{2}$ in × 6 in × 2 in (19 cm × 15 cm × 5 cm).
Eleanor Fielden

Scissor Case (Plates 29 and 30)
This box was made and lined in leather, so glueing was used instead of lacing. All the individual pieces were sewn together with ladder-stitch using nylon invisible thread.

29 Scissor case in grey gloving kid. 2¾in × 7¼in × 1¼in (7 cm × 18 cm × 3 cm)

30 Inside of scissor case with glued blue suede lining

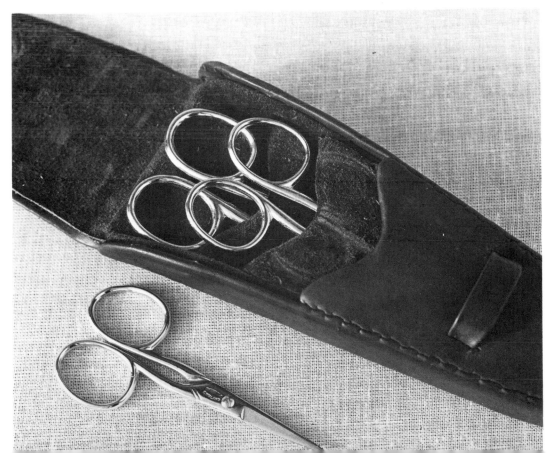

Domed Lids (Plate 31 and Plate 18, page 69)

The two boxes illustrated happen to be hexagons, but the principle is the same however many sides the box may have.

To construct the roof sections of the lid, the base of the triangle is drawn equal to the inside measurement of the side of the lip. From the middle of this line a perpendicular is drawn equal to the measurement from the side of the lip to the centre of the lid. This gives the point of the triangle (Fig. 92). If used like this, the triangular sections would form a flat lid. By lengthening the perpendicular, the lid begins to have a slope. The longer the perpendicular, the taller the dome will be (Fig. 93). Plate 32 shows the lid of the Jubilee Box in construction.

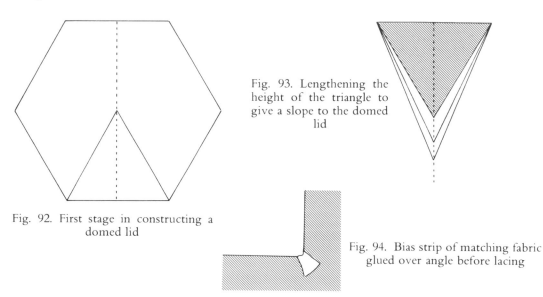

Fig. 93. Lengthening the height of the triangle to give a slope to the domed lid

Fig. 92. First stage in constructing a domed lid

Fig. 94. Bias strip of matching fabric glued over angle before lacing

Castellated or Shaped edges

The Jubilee Box had the problem of a castellated edge (Plate 32). By cutting the felt padding on the outside of the long lip $\frac{1}{8}$ in (3 mm) longer on the castellated edge, the wear by the thick card on the wild silk fabric was softened. As the silk was laced over the edge into position, the felt was also pulled over to cover the thickness of the card. This felt edge also served to give an extra layer to stitch to when the inside of the castellated edge was lined with antique silver leather (Plate 33).

The angles were an obvious problem since, if the silk had just been snipped into to allow it to be pulled over the edge for the purpose of lacing there would have been gaps and raw edges on all the inside angles of the castellation, due to the thickness of the card. To avoid this, small bias strips of matching fabric were glued over the angles (Fig. 94) before lacing the silk into position. In addition, the snipped angles in the silk were painted with glue to prevent fraying. When this was all firmly laced into position and the leather lining brought up and sewn to the top edge, the angles were extremely neat and no cut edge was discernible.

31 Jubilee box in wild silk. The castellated edge is lined with Persian leather. The overlapping lid extends to the base platform, which is covered in gloving suede. The domed lid is in purple velvet. 10 in × 10 in × 7 in (25 cm × 25 cm × 18 cm)

32 The lid of the Jubilee box in construction.

33 The outside of the Jubilee box represents the Queen's public life, with the cross representing her position as head of the Church of England. The 'jewels' in the crown are the coats-of-arms, badges or motifs of the members of the Commonwealth.

The inside of the box represents the Queen's private life. There are six compartments with their own individual drop-in lids, each showing initials or initial and a date. E and P for Elizabeth and Philip and the date of their wedding. E and P and the date of their Silver Wedding Anniversary. C for Charles and the date of his birth. A for Anne and the date of her birth and a lid each for Andrew and Edward

34 A close-up of the inside of the Jubilee box showing the central compartment which depicts the coat-of-arms of the House of Windsor

Alternative Shapes

There are many shapes that have not been covered in these sections (Plate 35), but I hope that an understanding of the construction of boxes will have been achieved and it will be found that each new shape and problem can be tackled, thought out and overcome without too many mistakes. Plate 36 shows how additional interest can be added to the rim of a lid.

35 Tortoise box with a patchwork base to the shell decorated with tortoiseshell beads, raffene, braid, various threads and leather.
11 in × 8 in × 5 in (28 cm × 20 cm × 13 cm)

36 Round flush-sided velvet box. The silk patchwork lid has a raised border over card. 11 in diameter × 5 in (28 cm diameter × 13 cm).
Valerie Harding

It is advisable always to make a cardboard mock-up when a new shape is being undertaken. In this way many problems are overcome before valuable time and fabric have been taken up.

CHAPTER THREE

Bags and Purses

Designing the Bag or Purse

The size of the bag or purse will depend on what it is going to be worn with or used for. An identical pattern can be made up in 6 in (15 cm) long or 14 in (35 cm) long and both will have their own uses. The height of the person who will own the bag must also be considered: a petite woman can be dwarfed by too large a handbag.

Different sized bags will require different quality and weight of fabric. A silk or satin clutch purse for the evening is usually small and neat, whilst a large shopper or all purpose carrier will be of more durable materials. Therefore it is important to settle on the use that the bag will be put to since this will determine the size and very likely the type of fabric required. Obviously the chosen embroidery technique will also influence the fabric.

Bags vary enormously with fashion (Plate 37), both in their proportions and in their type of finish. Sometimes they are stiff and hard, at other periods they are soft and spongy. This means that the type of interlining required is vital, not only to the way that the bag will stand up to wear and tear, but also for the fashion feel.

To help give a professional finish, it is often an asset to combine patterned material and embroidered sections, especially canvas work, with leather, suede or contrasting firm fabrics. This contrasting material can be used for the binding, piped edges, gussets, bases and handles, as the design demands. As these parts take most of the wear, they will not show the dirt as much if a darker tone than the main body of the bag is chosen. Using these firmer materials on the points of wear will also add strength to the bag.

The positioning of the embroidery is also an important decision. If a motif or small area of embroidery is being worked, it needs to be placed so that it is not hidden when the bag is carried. An area on the flap, if the bag has one, is a traditional position, as is a central area on the front of a bag without a flap.

Bags, whatever their size, can be divided into definite groups by the way that they are constructed.

37 This shows a variety of bags. Canvas bag with bamboo handle. *Dorothy Carbonell*. Velvet bag with gold-work, patchwork leather bag, macramé and suede bag. *Mary Greening*. Canvas tote bag. *Lois Hennequin*. Macramé pochette. *Mollie Ruthven*

Shapes without Gussets

These are the simplest type of all. Flat pieces are joined together with no additional strips being inserted to give depth.

Gussets in One Piece with the Sides

This is where the main pieces of the bag are cut or seamed in such a way that the gussets are formed without additional pieces being set in to give depth.

Soft Gussets

This is where strips of matching or companion fabrics are set into the side seams to add depth and give more space inside.

Stiff Gussets

In this type, the gussets are stiffened with heavy card to maintain the shape of the bag. They are more often found in the larger shoppers or travel bags.

Gussets Cut in One Piece with the Handle

This pattern has been used in recent years for the tote and casual bag. Handle and gusset are made of one continuous length of fabric, webbing or wide braid.

Gussets Cut in One Piece with the Base and the Handle
This type is similar to the previous shape, but this time the long strip forms the base of the bag as well as the gussets and handle. The long strip of fabric can be shaped to give greater width at the base. It is not necessary for it to remain the same width as the handle all the way round the bag.

Tools and Materials

Bags or purses can be made of any material, provided that a suitable interlining is used to bring them up to the required weight of fabric for the size of bag being made. It must be appreciated that some fabrics will not wear as well as others, but attractive bags can still be made as long as durability is not required in that particular case.

Interlinings

HEAVY CALICO This fabric will give body without rigidity to any material and is especially useful as a backing to a soft fabric like tweed, which is likely to stretch out of shape in use.

THIN CALICO A silky lining will carry the pockets better, keep its shape and be less likely to tear away from its stitching if it is backed by a light-weight calico.

VILENE BONDAWEB OR PELLON This is just an easy method of glueing the fabric to another interlining. By bonding a fine fabric or suede to a calico a crispness is obtained which is excellent for certain styles of bag. It ensures that stretchy materials, especially suedes and leathers, remain in shape during and after construction. Otherwise these fabrics can be extremely difficult to handle.

IRON-ON VILENE OR PELLON This interlining is available in different weights. It gives an even firmer base than the previous type, as the fabric is bonded direct to a stiffer interlining. It just depends how stiff a finish is required.

PELMET VILENE OR PELLON This is a heavy-weight Vilene which gives a real firmness to a bag. It is advisable to use a layer of calico, very thin foam rubber or a thin layer of wadding between pelmet Vilene and thin fabrics as otherwise it looks rather hard and mean.

FOAM RUBBER This can be obtained in various thicknesses from $\frac{1}{8}$ in (3 mm) upwards. The fine one is excellent to use under thin fabrics to add a bit of richness. The $\frac{1}{2}$ in (15 mm) or $\frac{3}{4}$ in (2 cm) give a good shape and resilience to a large bag or shopper.

BUCKRAM This is a very stiff and unsympathetic interlining, but is needed for a really stiff, hard bag. It would need some sort of wadding or thin foam rubber between it and the fabric to give a softer appearance.

TAILORS' CANVAS This wide range of interlining gives a variation of quality of stiffening, but it is very expensive to buy especially for a bag. It does the job very well if a remnant is available.

Wadding
Courtelle wadding is the nicest and easiest to use, either for quilting or to give a thin layer under a fine material that needs to have something to soften the look of the stiff interlining.

Boning
The boning is placed along the entire edge of the flaps, main pockets and folds to keep the bag rigid and in shape (Fig. 95). The modern polyester boning is available by the metre and does not need to have a tape casing to hold it, as it can be machined along its edges into the required positions on the interlining.

Fig. 95. Boning placed in position on the interlining for a clutch bag

Card
Stiff card can be used for stiffening the base of larger bags and shoppers and for making stiff gussets.

Medium-thick card, usually covered in thin leather or suede, is used to frame a piece of embroidery, the whole forming the front or the flap of a bag (Plate 38).

If rigid bags are in fashion, card can be used as an interlining, but it does look very hard and needs a thin layer of foam rubber or wadding placed between the card and the fabric to give it an acceptable appearance.

The problem about using card as an interlining is that it can crack with use and this shows through the fabric.

Tools
Paper, pencil, rubber, a good ruler, and set square are all needed for drawing out the pattern. Squared paper is very helpful if you have it, but it is not a necessity. Various sizes of scissors are needed. Glass-headed pins are very nice to use. Clothes pegs and large bulldog clips can be useful in some cases.

38 Green suede bag with a framed canvas-work inset. *Lois Hennequin*

Threads

You will need a matching thread to the fabric, tacking threads, coloured and white, invisible nylon thread (see page 36) and fine crochet cotton for any lacing that might be needed.

Needles

Normal sewing needles are adequate, suitable for the thread and fabric being used. A curved needle is occasionally required.

Finishes

In the same way that each bag shape or pattern can be made up in different sizes and fabrics, different finishes and details can be applied to suit the style of bag and give it individuality.

Simple Edge (Fig. 96)

The simplest method of all is to turn the fabrics back to the wrong side over the interlining and herringbone into place. The lining is then stitched into place to cover the raw edges.

This method is perfectly satisfactory as long as a firm fabric is used which will give a good sharp edge over the interlining, otherwise it may wear badly and become sloppy on the interlining.

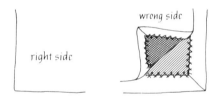

Fig. 96. Simple edge. Showing the right and wrong side. The turnings are herringboned back onto the interlinings

Piped Edge

This method gives a clean-cut framing to the embroidery and makes a very serviceable finish. The piping can be of the same material as the bag, or a contrasting colour and fabric (Plate 57, page 119). (For the method to cut and make piping see CUSHIONS, page 132.)

When choosing the string or cord that is to be covered to make the piping, do be careful that the finished piping will be in proportion to the bag or purse, as it can easily be bulky and clumsy.

The turnings of the piping on the inside of the bag can be finished with a facing so that the lining is set 1 in (3 cm) away from the piped edge (Fig. 97). Alternatively the lining can be set directly onto the stitch line of the piping (Fig. 98).

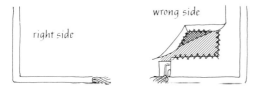

Fig. 97. Piped edge. Showing the right and wrong side. A facing is applied and the lining set in from the edge

Fig. 98. Piped edge. Showing the right and wrong side. The lining is set onto the stitch line of the piping

Bound Edges

This method gives a wider, firmer edge to the bag and can pull the embroidery and shape together visually. If a firm leather is being used for the binding, it can be top-stitched on with no turnings, either by machine or by stab-stitching the edge (Fig. 99). Although a soft leather or suede does not fray and can be stitched on like the thicker leathers, a very much sharper stitch line is achieved by applying it with a turning so that the machining does not show (Fig. 100 and Plate 49). This also applies to a cross woven silk or wool braid which, without experience, can give a very wobbly edge when sewn on either by hand or machine top stitching.

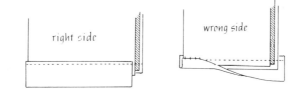

Fig. 99. Bound edge. Top stitched with no turning to the binding

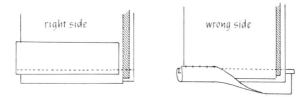

Fig. 100. Bound edge. Binding applied with a turning

Inset Behind a Frame (Plate 38, page 93)

A canvas-work bag can be given a much smarter appearance by combining it with leather or suede. One of the methods of doing this is to cover thick card with leather, leaving a hole to frame the canvas-work. Obviously the size and shape of the hole is dictated by the shape of the bag. If material other than leather is used for the frame, do remember that to achieve a neat appearance, enough stretch is needed in the fabric to pull it right round the edge of the frame to the wrong side. Otherwise the fabric round the hole needs to have an applied facing to give a good finish. Naturally, embroidery techniques other than canvas-work can be set behind a frame.

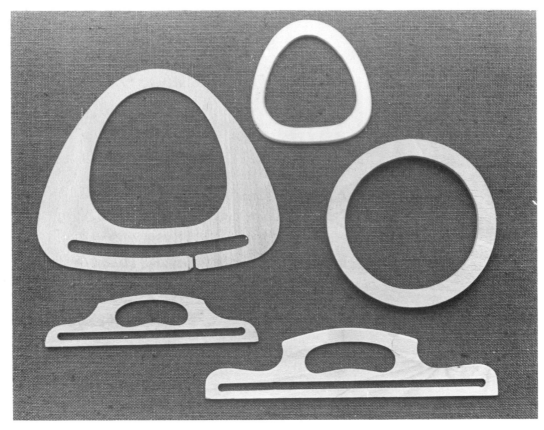

39 Three different types of commercial wooden handles in different sizes

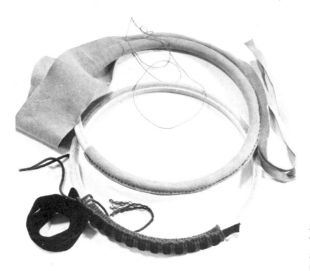

40 Two wooden ring handles being covered. The first with grey suede, and the second with a velvet ribbon woven into a cord made over the ring in a macramé string. $6\frac{1}{4}$ in (16 cm) diameter

A   Islamic design in gold-work on a chest of drawers. $8\frac{1}{2}$ in × $5\frac{1}{4}$ in × $4\frac{3}{4}$ in (20 cm × 14 cm × 12 cm).

B The Jubilee box was presented to Her Majesty the Queen on the occasion of her Silver Jubilee by the National Federation of Womens' Institutes. 10 in × 10 in × 7 in (25 cm × 25 cm × 18 cm).

C Café curtains with a scalloped heading made from black and white ticking. The toadstools are applied with Bondaweb and edged with a machine zig-zag couched thread.

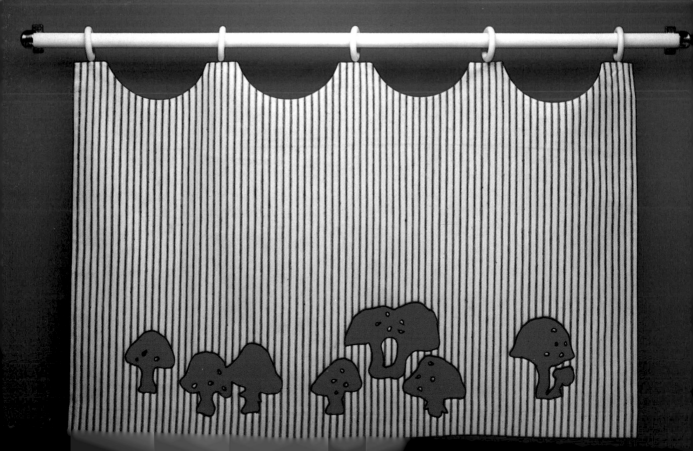

Handles

Various handles are on the market, but a bought handle is inclined to dictate the shape and size of a bag and this gives them a limited use.

Cane handles (Plate 37, page 90) do well on summer bags and beach bags. Plastic ring handles serve the same purpose, but do not always have the same character.

Wooden handles come in three main shapes and a variety of sizes (Plate 39). If they are to be plain, they should be sandpapered and sealed with one of the many polyurethane wood finishes. They are made in different colour wood dyes and the primary colours. Several coats are needed to build up a good finish. Naturally the handles can be painted with an oil-based paint if it suits the design of the bag, but personally I think that wood sealers are more attractive.

There is only a limited use for wood-finished handles and they have more style and a smarter appearance when covered. Plate 40 shows round handles being covered, the first by suede being top-stitched round it with the surplus suede being trimmed away afterwards. The second handle has two lengths of macramé string cording a Solomon's Knot over a core of the wooden ring and a length of velvet ribbon. The velvet ribbon is placed alternately above and below the knotting (Fig. 101).

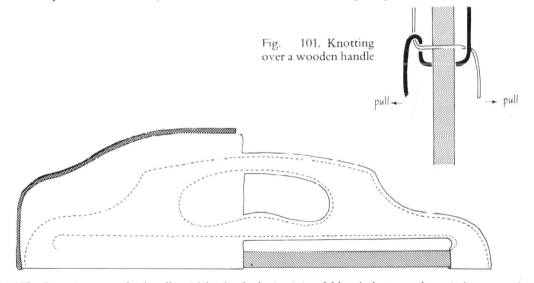

Fig. 101. Knotting over a wooden handle

pull ←   → pull

Fig. 102. Covering a wooden handle with leather by laying it in a fold at the bottom edge, stitching round and cutting the surplus away

Plate 41 shows another handle covered with leather. The leather is first stab-stitched round the outside of the handle and trimmed, then stab-stitched on the inside of the handle and the surplus leather cut away. Finally, the slit which carries the fabric of the bag is stitched on the upper edge of the hole. The leather is then cut with a Stanley knife below the stitching (Fig. 102). There is rarely room to do a second row of stitching through the slit of the handle and the raw wood on the lower side of the slit is covered by the fabric passing through the hole.

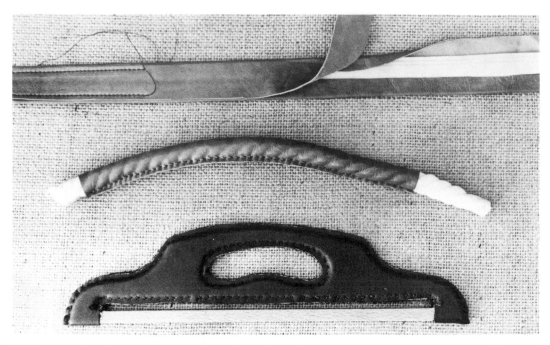

41 Three handles. Leather covering a petersham ribbon, leather over a piping cord and leather folded and stitched round a commercial wooden handle

Handles can be made of plaited leathers or fabric. Twisted cords of varying thicknesses are made out of string or any yarn suitable for the purpose. Plate 42 shows a twisted rope handle made out of a coarse garden twine for a plastic-lined scrim beach bag.

Plate 41 shows leather stitched over thick upholstery cord to give a very serviceable handle, which is comfortable to hold. The same photograph shows stiff petersham ribbon being covered by leather to make a flat handle. The leather is folded round the petersham and edge-stitched with a machine, then a flat strip of leather is glued on the back to cover the join.

Webbing which is manufactured for saddlers or upholsterers makes excellent handles, especially for tote bags, where the webbing also forms the side gusset (Plate 60, page 122) and occasionally the base as well.

Matching fabric can always make the handles too, but it is important that it has sufficient interlining to give it strength and to prevent any stretching or distortion.

Plate 59, page 120 shows handles of Bargello canvas-work. These are strong and an integral part of the overall design.

Plate 47, page 107, is a small, double-sided purse with ordinary household chain making the handle. This chain is available with a brass or chrome finish.

The commercial metal-frame tops with clip fastenings either have a chain handle already attached or a fitting to take a fabric handle. Like the commercial wooden handles, they are constricting in the choice of design for the bag.

Attaching Handles

A PLAIT OR GROUP OF THIN CORDS These can be knotted and kept in place by a band of matching material just above the knot (Fig. 103).

Fig. 103. A group of thongs knotted and attached to the bag by a band of leather

A CHAIN This can have a fold of fabric passed through the last link. If a binding is being used, this can be left a little longer and can hold the chain into position (Plate 47, page 107).

42 Scrim beach bag lined with plastic. Machine embroidery decoration and a garden twine cord handle. $16\frac{1}{2}$ in × 17 in (42 cm × 43 cm)

'D' RING Most handles look well folded over a 'D' ring which is held in place by a strap (Plate 57, page 119) or by a shaped piece.

Fasteners

It is possible to obtain from saddlers, cobblers and leather suppliers various brass or chrome fasteners to hold the bag flap in position, but so often this type will conflict with the embroidery. A concealed press stud is often the best answer, but these do need a special tool to set them in the fabric. If this type is used, the upper half should be set onto the lining and lining interlining before the lining is attached to the main bag, otherwise the head of the press stud will have to show on the outside of the bag.

Various dressmaking fasteners can be used for bags. Very large press studs and Velcro fastening are suitable, but care needs to be taken that a good finish is achieved and the result does not look 'home-made' in the worst sense! The press studs should always be sewn on with buttonhole stitch, with the same number of stitches to each hole to give a neat finish. Using $\frac{1}{4}$-in (5-mm) magnets as fasteners has been tried, but they tend to be bulky.

A fastener is really unnecessary if the bag flap is long enough, as it is held down by its own weight. But if for safety reasons a fastener is required, then a zip fastener across the top of the large compartment is a neat and practical answer (Fig. 104).

Innumerable buttons, toggles, ties and loops can be evolved (Plate 43), but it is most important that they are an integral part of the embroidery design. Very often they can form the focal point and the design builds up to them (Plates 44 and 45).

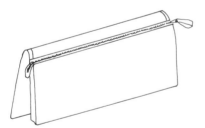

Fig. 104. A zip fastener across the pocket of a clutch bag

43 A sampler of fasteners

44 Shoulder bag with textured embroidery on linen with toggle fastener. 9 in × 7 in (23 cm × 18 cm). *Eileen Cottle*

45 The same bag open to show marbled lining and purse

Drawing out the Pattern

In this section on bags, no patterns with detailed measurements are given, merely shapes. This is because fashion in proportion and shape of bags and purses changes with each season and different size bags suit different size people.

The best result to suit an individual can be achieved by drawing out a suggested shape in stiff paper, cutting it out, then holding it in front of a mirror to see how the size and proportions suit you. It is well worth while taking a great deal of trouble in this planning stage as even 1 in (3 cm) can make all the difference.

Always use a sharp pencil, set square and good ruler. If a curved shape is being drawn out, establish the size and approximate shape first; then, choosing the side which has got the best line and curve, fold the pattern in half and trace the line onto the second side. It may well have to be drawn out onto a second piece of paper before it can be properly corrected. Be certain to mark the centre line and check that the pattern is equal on both sides.

If the bag has a front flap, it is necessary to give some extra length to it in order to allow additional depth at the top of the bag for when it is filled. This may not be apparent in a flat pattern, especially on a pochette or clutch-purse style.

When cutting out the fabric, do remember that no seam allowances have been made and these must be added on right round the paper pattern.

Order of Work

This résumé is intended to help with the making of all types of bags, but it is essential to have read the detailed methods and techniques in the following sections before actually beginning the first attempt.

1. Plan the use, size, shape, gusset style, embroidery, finish, handle and handle fixing, fastener, fabric, interlining, lining and fittings.
2. Cut out paper pattern.
3. Cut out main fabric with 1-in (3-cm) seam allowance all round and work the embroidered areas. Make sure that the grain is correct and tack in a centre line.
4. Select an interlining to suit the chosen fabric and the style of the bag. Cut interlining $\frac{1}{8}$ in (3 mm) smaller than the original paper pattern on all edges.
5. If boning is needed, machine it into position on a suitable interlining.
6. Cut out lining as paper pattern with $\frac{1}{2}$-in (15-mm) seam allowance all round. Should the bag be a gathered style, then a lining without gathers may be required, in which case a new pattern will have to be drawn out for it.
7. Cut the interlining for the lining $\frac{1}{8}$ in (3 mm) smaller on all sides than the bag paper pattern. This may need to be trimmed down later depending on the style of bag.
8. Cut the gussets in fabric plus seam allowance.
   Cut the gusset interlining $\frac{1}{8}$ in (3 mm) smaller on all sides.
   Cut the gusset lining and lining interlining.
9. Cut the fabric, interlining and stiffening for the base.
   Cut any additional base lining.
10. Tack main bag fabric to the interlining.
    Herringbone the interlining to the fabric as required by the pattern.
    Put on any metal stud feet required.
    Stitch on piping, if it is the chosen finish.
11. Make any pockets required for the outside of the bag and stitch on.
12. Make and attach any handles required.
13. Make and attach the fastener.
14. Depending on the pattern of the bag, make up the gussets independently, or machine gusset pieces to main bag shape.
15. Check the measurements for the bag lining.
    Trim the lining interlining as necessary.
    Herringbone the interlining to the lining as required.
16. Make and attach all inside fittings to the lining and interlining.
17. Tack lining to main part of bag if it is to have a bound edge.
    Ladder-stitch all other linings into position.
18. Bind edges as required by the pattern.
19. Where both the gussets and the base are stiff, i.e. of thick card, it is impossible to turn the bag inside out once it is made up. The sides and base have to be completed, the gussets completed and then all ladder-stitched together into position from the right side.

Shapes Without Gussets

Many pochette or clutch bags are this shape; small, neat envelope purses that are made to match an evening dress or outfit (Fig. 105). Various shaped purses hung from belts or round the neck, are also mostly made without gussets (Plate 46). Some are gathered-up circles (Fig. 106) others are a flat bag with a thong threaded through the neck (Fig. 107), but often they are the flat envelope shape.

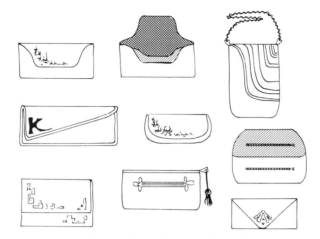

Fig. 105. Shapes for pochettes and clutch bags

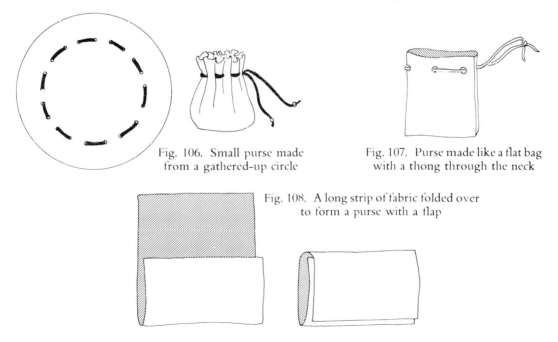

Fig. 106. Small purse made from a gathered-up circle

Fig. 107. Purse made like a flat bag with a thong through the neck

Fig. 108. A long strip of fabric folded over to form a purse with a flap

Clutch Bag
The simplest of all is a strip of fabric folded over to make a purse with a flap (Fig. 108).

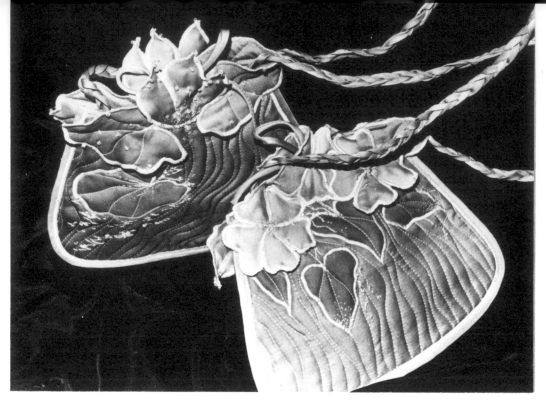

46 A pair of painted silk quilted purses with appliqued flowers and plaited handles. *Susan Rangeley*

CUTTING OUT THE BAG Cut out the paper pattern and trace its shape onto the selected fabric. Work any embroidery at this stage. This may give a calico backing to the embroidery, which can be used as an interlining, but an additional layer will probably be required to give more body and to carry the boning.

INTERLINING AND BONING A dressmaking weight of Vilene, a thick calico or $\frac{1}{8}$ in (3 mm) foam rubber all make suitable interlinings. Anything stiffer or heavier is normally unsuitable for this size of bag. If something extra is required to make sure that it will keep its shape, then boning is the answer. Modern polyester dressmaking boning is easy to handle and can be machined along its edge to fasten it to a calico or Vilene interfacing (Fig. 95, page 92). If there is no boning available, strips cut from a plastic bleach or washing-up liquid bottle will serve very well on a small bag. They will need to be set into a tape casing to hold them in position. The tape is stitched onto the interlining first and then the plastic strips are inserted.

SIMPLE EDGE (Fig. 96, page 94), PIPED EDGE (Figs 97 and 98, page 95) AND BOUND EDGE (Figs 99 and 100, page 95) The interlining is cut $\frac{1}{8}$ in (3 mm) smaller than the paper pattern and herringboned onto the fabric (Fig. 109) so that it does not show on the right side. The seam allowance on the end that will form the top of the pocket is then turned over onto the wrong side, pressed with an iron and herringboned onto the interlining (Fig. 110).

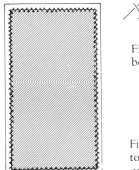

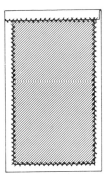

Fig. 109. The interlining herring-boned into position on the wrong side of the fabric

Fig. 110. The seam allowance of the top edge of the pocket is turned over and herringboned on the interlining

SIMPLE EDGE Fold the bag into position with the right side inside, then pin and tack the seams ready for stitching from A to B and F to E (Fig. 111). For leather, suede and velvet, it will be found helpful to tack with an oversewing stitch, which prevents movements while stitching.

Fig. 111. The bag folded into position inside out ready to stitch from A to B, and F to E

PIPED EDGE If the bag is to have a piped finish, piping needs to be prepared that is long enough to run from the pocket corner A, up the seam to B, round the flap B to C to D to E, then down the seam E to the corner at F (Fig. 111). (For the method of making piping see CUSHIONS, page 132.)

If a narrow facing is to be set to the piping on the flap, before the application of the lining (Fig. 97, page 95), it can be pinned in with the piping and all seamed together with one line of stitching. Otherwise the lining can be set to the piping (Fig. 98, page 95) and no facing is required.

TIDYING THE POCKET Press the seam flat on the wrong side and trim the turnings so that they are of unequal widths, which prevents them being bulky. Snip into the turning at the top edge of the pocket (Fig. 112) to allow the turnings on the flap to be brought over onto the interlining. Mitre the top corners of the flap (Fig. 8, page 24) and herringbone the turnings flat onto the interlining, having first pressed the edge with an iron (Fig. 113). Turn the pocket through to the right side and press again. Make sure that the seam has a really sharp, crisp edge.

HANDLES AND FASTENINGS These should be attached to the main body of the bag before the lining is inserted, so that no stitching shows on the inside.

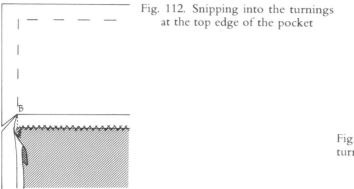

Fig. 112. Snipping into the turnings
at the top edge of the pocket

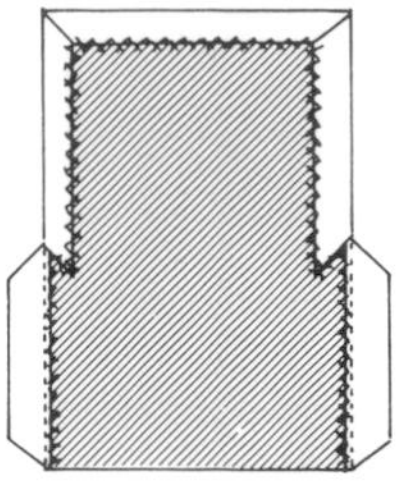

Fig. 113. Reverse of bag, showing the
turnings of the flap herringboned into
position on the interlining

LINING The lining is interlined with a thin calico to take the weight of the fittings, pockets, etc. The lining fabric also wears much better on the edges of the flap and pocket when it is interlined, and the stitching is less likely to rip away.

Should the bag still feel a little floppy when the lining comes to be made up, extra body can be given to the whole bag by interlining with felt.

Cut the lining as the paper pattern with $\frac{1}{2}$-in (15-mm) seam allowance all round. The interlining is cut $\frac{1}{8}$ in (3 mm) smaller on all sides than the paper pattern and it may need to be trimmed a little later on, depending on the method chosen for finishing the bag.

Tack the lining to the interlining. All the lining fittings need to be made onto the lining at this stage, before it is attached to the main fabric (see Linings and Fittings, page 124).

Fold the lining into position and pin up the side seams so that the interlining is just caught by $\frac{1}{8}$ in (3 mm) and drop it into the main bag in order to adjust the size. The lining needs to fit the pocket opening of the bag exactly, otherwise there are unsightly gathers if it is too big and gaps at the seams if the lining is too small. The pins marking the proposed seams on the lining can be adjusted to make sure that it is an exact fit. Stitch the seams, press and return the lining to the bag. Pin the lining along the edge of the pocket. The lining can now be pinned to the edge of the flap. The lining and interlining may need to be trimmed if the lining is set back from the edge of the flap. The lining requires a turning, but the interlining should lie flat. When the lining is sewn into position, the thread catches the edge of the interlining as well as the fold of lining and holds them both firm.

BOUND EDGE The seam allowance on the end of the lining that will meet the edge of the pocket on the main bag is turned over onto the wrong side, pressed and herringboned onto its interlining. The lining is then placed onto the wrong side of the main bag, against the interlining (Fig. 114). Tack the pieces together all round the edge. The lining can be ladder-stitched to the pocket edge of the bag.

Fold the bag over to form the pocket with the lining on the inside and pin the seams (Fig. 115). Tack the seams. Prepare a length of binding, with or without turnings as required (Figs 99 and 100, page 95). The binding will need to be as long as the piping in Fig. 111.

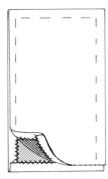

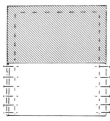

Fig. 115. The bag folded and pinned with the lining on the inside ready to be bound

Fig. 114. The lining being laid on the wrong side of the bag in preparation for a bound edge

Double-Sided Purse (Plates 47 and 48)

This is a charming little pattern, which makes up well in a firm cotton. Two purses are made up back to back, so that there is also a pocket between the two backs. The outsides can well be patchwork or quilting, but the insides need to be thin fabric, otherwise it is very bulky when the edges are bound. It is important to have a contrasting lining as this gives added interest.

The handle can be matching fabric, cord or chain, as in this example.

In this bag, each piece was fused to its lining with Bondaweb, which gave a certain crispness and made the pieces easier to handle.

47 Double-sided purse with a bound edge and chain handle. $6\frac{1}{2}$ in × $7\frac{3}{4}$ in (16 cm × 19 cm)

48 The same purse showing the flap raised

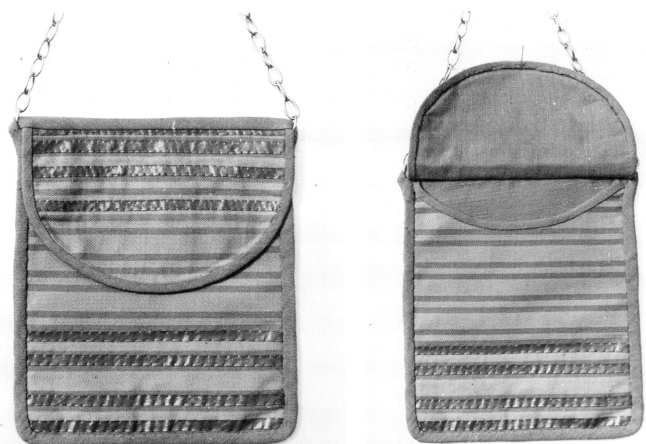

TO MAKE UP (Fig. 116) Tack or Bondaweb each piece of lining to its main piece of fabric, so that it can be handled as one piece of fabric, 1a on 1, etc.

Bind the curve of the two purse flaps A to B.

Bind the pocket edges of the two purses C to D.

Lay piece 2 onto piece 1, with linings face to face. Lay pocket flap 3 on top and bind along the top edge E to F.

Repeat for Front purse.

Lay the two purses back to back and bind down the side, round the base and up the sides E to G to H to F to hold the purses together.

The ends of the binding that has just been put on will not only neaten the ends of the binding from E to F, but can be used to hold the handle in position. This bag would enlarge well made up in a deck-chair canvas or heavy drill.

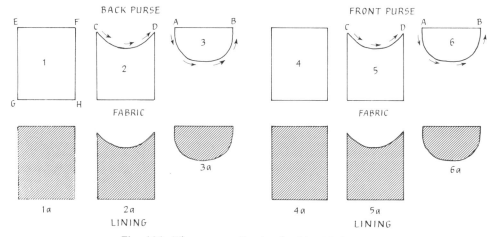

Fig. 116. The pattern for the double-sided purse

Fold-over Bag

The bag shown in Plates 49 and 50 has the same pattern as the bag whose interior is shown in Plate 51, but due to their different materials, size and proportions, they have totally different characters. Basically, they are one long rectangle of fabric that is interlined and lined, then folded over to form a bag. The edges are bound; then it is folded in half again to carry as a pochette or clutch bag.

If quilting or any very textured type of technique is being used, it is advisable to apply it to only half the length of fabric and to use a plain, untreated fabric for the second half, which will form the inside of the fold-over.

In Plate 51, velvet ribbon was used for the outside of the bag and a silky fabric with a slub weave for the inside of the fold-over, to give a less bulky finish.

In Plate 50 the suede with the light machine quilting was carried right through the strip, so that it is on the inside as well as the outside of the fold.

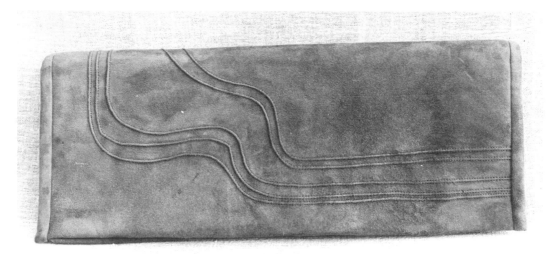

49 Soft suede fold-over bag with a bound edge. $13\frac{1}{2}$ in $\times$ $5\frac{1}{2}$ in (34 cm $\times$ 14 cm)

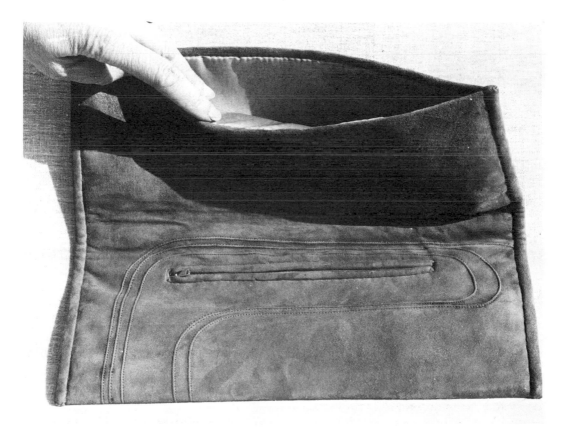

50 The same bag unfolded, showing the internal pocket and the inset zipped pocket

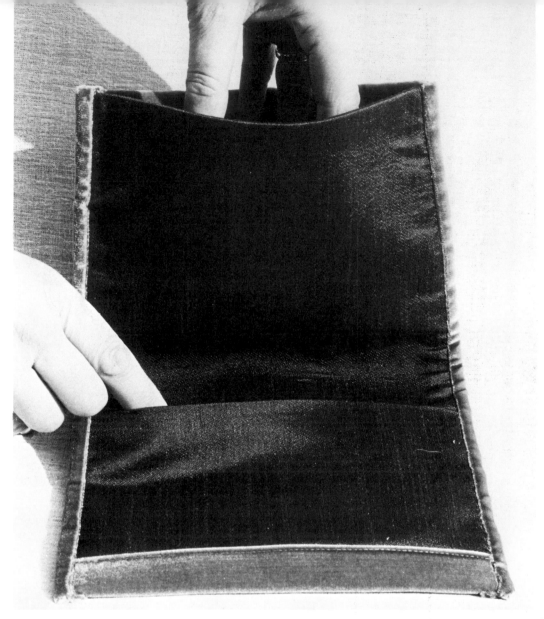

51 Fold-over bag made in velvet ribbons shown unfolded to reveal the dupion second side with the internal and external pockets

TO MAKE UP (Figs 117–122) Cut the length of fabric (Fig. 117) which is four times G to H (Fig. 122) plus 2 in (5 cm).

Cut the interlining and lining the same width, but $1\frac{1}{2}$ in (4 cm) shorter. The lining referred to below denotes the actual lining fabric plus a thin calico as a lining interlining.

Lay the interlining onto the main fabric which will be $\frac{3}{4}$ in (2 cm) longer at each end. Turn the $\frac{3}{4}$ in (2 cm) down over the interlining and herringbone into position. Press.

An inserted zipped pocket (Fig. 118) or an outside pocket (Fig. 119) is made at this stage if required (see INSERTED ZIPPED POCKET, page 125, or FLAT POCKET, page 124).

Fig. 117. Fold-over bag. The fabric, interlining and the lining (on top) cut in preparation

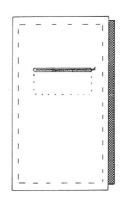

Fig. 118. The position of the inserted zipped pocket as shown in Plate 72

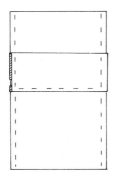

Fig. 119. The position of the additional outside pocket as shown in Plate 74

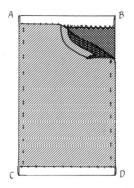

Fig. 120. The lining laid onto the interlined fabric and hemmed

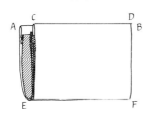

Fig. 121. Folding the strip in half to form a pocket ready for binding

Fig. 122. The bag folded over into its carrying position

Lay the lining onto the interlining and turn in $\frac{1}{2}$ in (15 mm) on the two ends and hem into position (Fig. 120).

Fold the piece in half so that A meets C and B meets D. Bind AC to E and DB to F (Fig. 121).

Be careful that the outside edge of the pocket being formed is fractionally longer than the inside edge when pinning and tacking in preparation for binding. Otherwise when the bag is folded over into its carrying position (Fig. 122), the back half of the pocket hangs down and shows the inside and the lining.

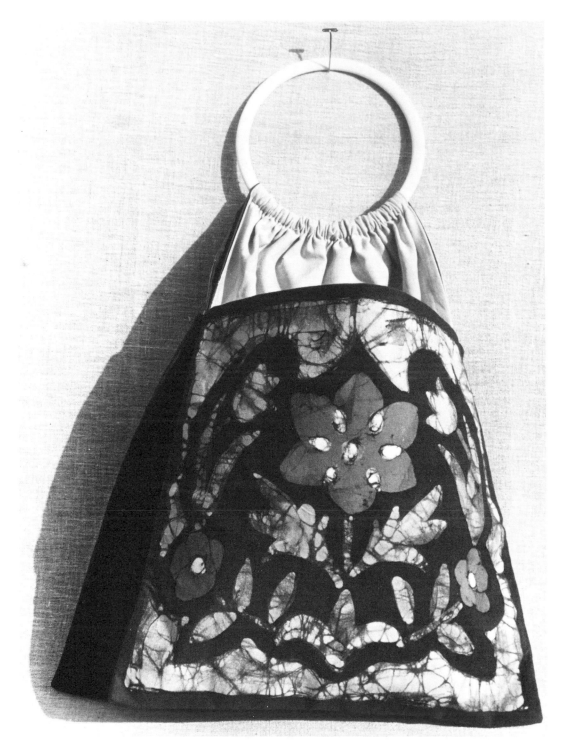

52 Batik summer bag. 12 in × 18 in (31 cm × 46 cm). *Kathleen Anderson*

Batik Bag (Plate 52)
This very simple shape makes an attractive summer or tote bag.

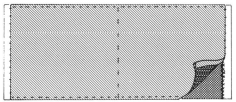

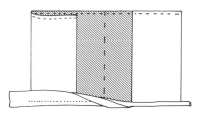

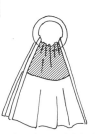

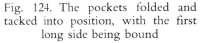

Fig. 123. Fabric, interlining and lining prepared for making up

Fig. 124. The pockets folded and tacked into position, with the first long side being bound

Fig. 125. The bag folded in half through the ring and stitched into position

TO MAKE UP (Figs 123–125) Cut a long strip of fabric, interlining and lining and lay them together. Neaten the two narrow ends by turning the fabric over onto the interlining and herringboning into position, then turning in the lining and hemming over the raw edge.

Mark the centre line where the handle will fold the strip in half.

Fold one narrow end up to form a pocket, tack into position (Fig. 124).

Repeat for the second end, checking that the pockets are of equal measurements.

Bind the full length of the long sides to neaten and make the pockets (Fig. 124).

Thread the fabric through a large ring handle. Make sure that the handle is lying on the centre line. Sew through the two layers of fabric on either side of the ring to keep it in position (Fig. 125).

Beach Towel Carry-all
The Batik bag pattern adapts beautifully to an all purpose beach bag.

TO MAKE UP (Figs 126 and 127) Using a good thick beach towel, mark the centre across the width and machine on a 2-in (5-cm) strip of matching tape. Thread through this channel a double length of cotton cord, making a loop and a tassel at both ends. The two loops make it easy to carry and the tassels prevent the cord from being pulled out of the channel.

Turn up each end of the towel to make two pockets (Fig. 127). Instead of sewing up these side seams, insert an open-ended plastic zip from A to B and similarly on the other three pocket seams. These can then be zipped up to carry things to and from the beach and unzipped to make the towel available for drying with or lying on.

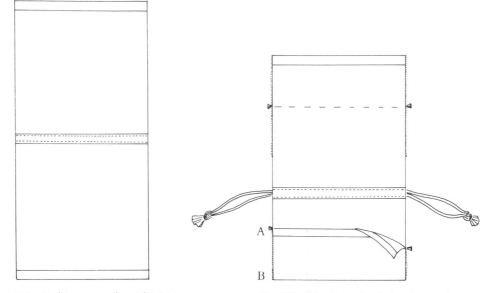

Fig. 126. Bathing towel with 2-in (5-cm) width tape stitched across the middle

Fig. 127. The four zips being inserted to make the pockets

Gussets Cut in One Piece with the Sides

There are two methods of giving a bag extra volume without adding in a separate gusset.

1. By cutting additional width to the pocket of the bag, which is then folded back inside to give the required depth.
2. By careful seaming so that gussets are formed out of flat sections.

Method 1
This method is seen in the clutch or pochette type of bag.

Fig. 128 shows the extra width allowed on the sides of the pocket to make the gusset. Do remember to leave seam allowances.

It depends on the weight of the fabric and interlining used as to whether the interlining is taken through to back the gusset, or ends on the edge of the pocket shape.

A calico will strengthen most gussets sufficiently without making them uncomfortably stiff. In the majority of cases, if a bag is interlined with heavy vilene it would be too stiff to use in the gussets and make this type of bag very bulky.

If bones are used, they should only lie on the main body of the bag and not extend into the gussets as they will prevent them folding inwards to the proper position.

There is always a danger point at the right angle between the top of the gusset and the edge of the bag flap (Fig. 129). For this reason, the best results with this pattern are obtained by facing the edge of the flap and the back gusset extension, with or without a piping. A 2-in (5-cm) facing is quite sufficient and the lining is laid onto this.

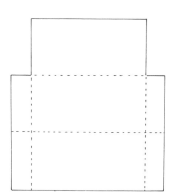

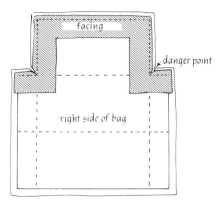

Fig. 128. Pattern for a bag with gussets cut in one piece with the sides

Fig. 129. The facing stitched into position before turning through to the wrong side of the bag

Having faced the flap and back gusset, fold over and herringbone the turnings to the interlining on the front of the pocket and front gusset. Fold the bag into shape, inside out and pin and machine the gusset seams together. Leave the bag inside out for mounting the lining.

The lining is prepared on its interlining and laid into position on the bag. Pin all the corners and straight edges. Now fold the flap over into its natural position to check if the lining is correctly placed or needs to be tightened up and made a little shorter.

The lining is laid round the gusset seams and sewn into position by hand. This is so much neater than matching them up first and then having bulky seams all meeting in the gusset edge. Before finally sewing, turn the bag through to the right side out and check that the lining really is sitting correctly.

Naturally, this type of bag can have a simple finish, a piping, or be bound as with the clutch bag.

53 Heavy calico bag bound in silk braid. 13½ in × 10 in (34 cm × 25 cm)

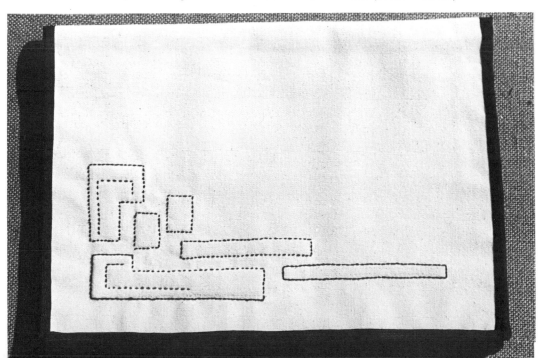

Method 2 (Plate 53)

The carefully placed seaming of flat pieces provides the bag with great spaciousness (Plate 54). Fig. 130 shows the pattern.

Pieces A, B and C fold in half to give a fold on the pocket edge. This means that each piece is self-lined.

Piece D forms the back and the flap and will be bound all the way round so it can be two separate lengths instead of a folded length.

Piece D is normally twice the depth of the pocket, to form the back of the pocket and then to fall forwards and provide the flap. If it is required that the bottom edge of the flap should lie level with the bottom edge of the pocket, do remember to allow at least 1–2 in (3–5 cm) extra for the depth of the bag when the pocket is filled. This depends on the size of bag being made.

TO MAKE UP Embroider D as required.

Apply iron-on Vilene to A, B, C, and D, or Bondaweb one half of each piece to the second half if a double thickness of fabric is stiff enough.

Fold each piece on the fold lines and press.

Stitch B and C together through all four thicknesses, approximately 2 in (5 cm) from the edge. This gives the width of the gusset and provides a small pocket. The gusset width is the main measurement to decide on, the pocket is incidental (Fig. 131).

54 The same bag open to show the great depth acquired by careful seaming

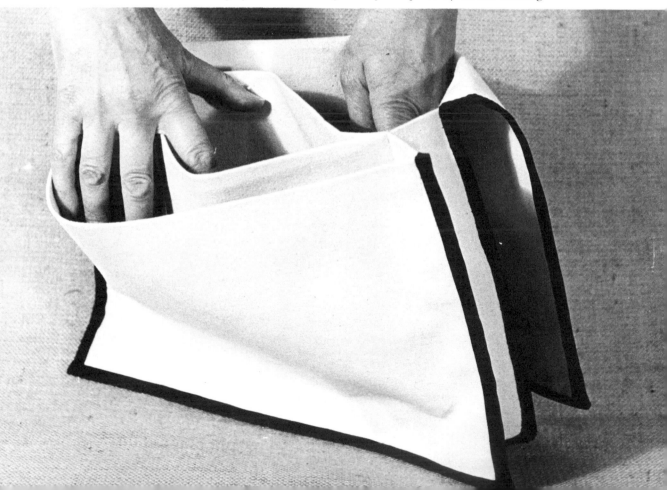

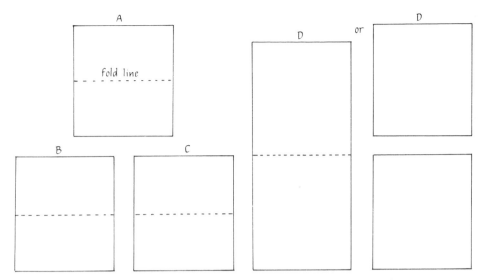

Fig. 130. The pattern for the calico bag bound with navy silk braid (Plate 77)

Fig. 131. B and C being machined together to give the gusset width and to provide a small pocket

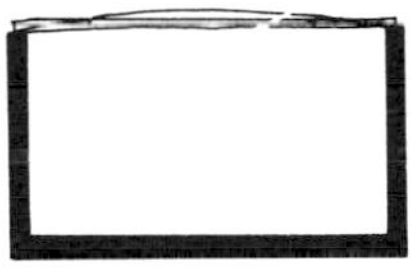

Fig. 132. A laid onto B; A and B bound together

Fig. 134. A rounded and a square based gusset

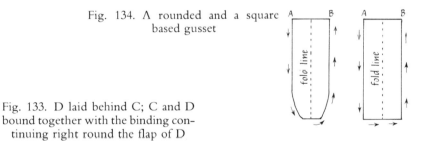

Fig. 133. D laid behind C; C and D bound together with the binding continuing right round the flap of D

A is now laid onto B; A and B are bound together (Fig. 132).

D is then laid behind C; C and D are bound together with the binding continuing right round the flap of D (Fig. 133). Check that the binding join is on the back of the bag and not on the flap.

Soft Gussets (Plate 55)

These are sections added into the sides of the pochette, clutch or envelope bags to give depth. They can have a rounded or square base (Fig. 134) depending on the shape of the bag required.

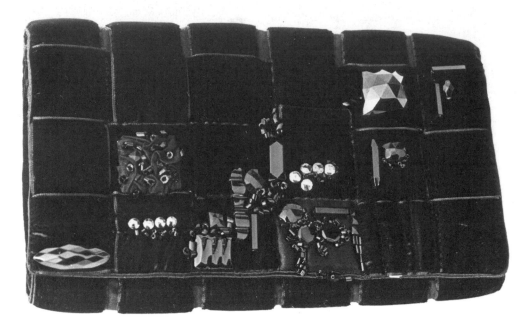

55 Black velvet ribbon pochette decorated with jet beads. 10 in × 6½ in (25 cm × 16 cm)

56 Quilted summer bag with applied leather. Soft gusset and base cut in one piece. Stiff card base made into the lining. 12 in × 12 in (31 cm × 31 cm). *Lucy Judd*

57 Canvas work with applied fabrics and leather on Winchester Canvas. Piped suede. 17 in × 8½ in (42 cm × 21 cm). *Designed by Jane Lemon, canvas worked by Sara Getley*

The alternative type of soft gusset can give the bag its very character as in a cylindrical bag (Plate 57).

Pochette, Clutch or Envelope Bag

The width of the gusset is not more than 3 in (7 cm) and very often only 1 or 1½ in (3 or 4 cm) wide. The measurement (Fig. 134) from A to B round the length of the gusset equals double the height of the bag plus the desired depth.

For smaller bags, the interlining on the gusset does not want to be as heavy as the main body of the bag, otherwise it will be too bulky and not fold flat. The interlining is cut ⅛ in (3 mm) smaller than the pattern as before and herringboned into position on the fabric. For a larger bag with narrow gussets, bones can be inserted into the interlining if desired (Fig. 135).

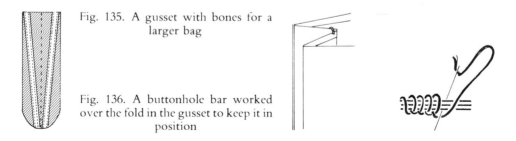

Fig. 135. A gusset with bones for a larger bag

Fig. 136. A buttonhole bar worked over the fold in the gusset to keep it in position

The gusset is seamed into the bag and then the turnings are turned back onto their own interlining and herringboned down to eliminate any bulk. Gussets which are required to fold inwards to flatten should be pressed on the wrong side, the fold pinched and a buttonhole bar worked to encourage them to turn inwards (Fig. 136).

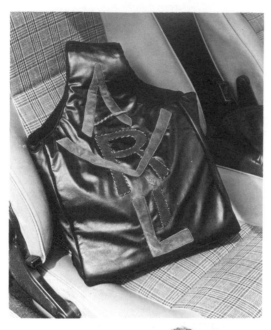

58 Black leather bag with applied leather and metal work initials. This soft bag is interlined with foam rubber. 12 in × 18 in (30 cm × 46 cm).
Mollie Collins

59 Corduroy shopper with Florentine canvas work handles. The gussets and base are interlined with thick card, and it has stud feet. 17½ in × 13½ in (43 cm × 34 cm). *Canvas worked by Molly Lance*

D Assorted garden cushions with patchwork motifs.
16 in × 16 in (41 cm × 41 cm). *Sara Getley*.

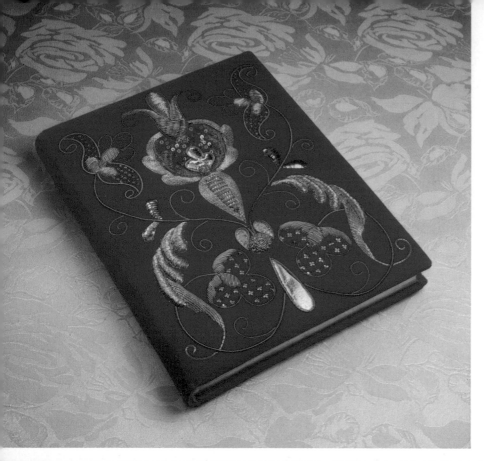

E Gold-work on velvet to make a professionally bound cover for a volume on Elizabethan embroidery. *Mollie Collins*.

F Mid-Wessex box with patchwork lid lining and quilted linings to tray compartments.

For a bag of the size of the cylindrical bag, although still a soft gusset, the same interlining is usually used for both the body of the bag and the gusset. This particular bag was worked on Winchester canvas and interlined with calico. As it was a big bag, the calico was machined into the seams with the canvas, instead of being taken up to the seams and then herringboned into place. This gave the extra strength necessary for its size.

Stiff Gussets

Large Shoppers

These are often more useful if they are free standing with stiff gussets and a stiff base (Plate 59). The gussets on this corduroy bag are shaped (Fig. 137) and interlined with thick card.

The gussets and the main body of the bag have to be prepared independently and made up at the end, because it is impossible to turn a bag inside out that has both a stiff base and stiff gussets.

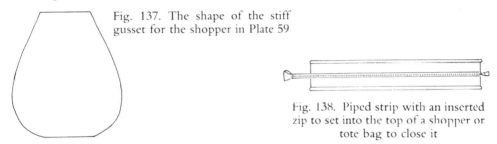

Fig. 137. The shape of the stiff gusset for the shopper in Plate 59

Fig. 138. Piped strip with an inserted zip to set into the top of a shopper or tote bag to close it

GUSSETS The card is cut (see GENERAL CONSTRUCTION, page 21) and padded with felt. The corduroy gusset is laced over it and the prepared piping is ladder-stitched into position round the edge.

The gusset lining is then prepared with a calico interlining and ladder-stitched onto the card base.

MAIN BAG The body of the bag is prepared next. This particular one was interlined with ¼ in (5 mm) foam rubber.

In this design, the handles go all round the bag and take the weight, so they are made up and stitched on next. The handles also serve to conceal the raw edges at the sides of the pocket, the bottom edge of which is turned over and stitched on the underside of the base.

The card is cut for the base and attached to the corduroy through the interlining, by four stud feet. These are placed 1 in (3 cm) from each corner.

The body of the bag is then lined before ladder-stitching to the gussets from the outside.

This particular bag has an open top, but two strips with a zip and piping finish could easily be made and attached if required (Fig. 138). The zip should be 2 in (5 cm) longer than the opening for easy access.

Gussets Cut in One Piece with the Handle (Plate 60)

This type makes very good tote bags of all sizes. The handle and gusset can be made of a contrasting webbing or leather, or of matching fabric. Whatever is chosen must be firm and strong, or well interlined. Nothing is worse than a soft, stretched handle that creases into a fold.

This style of bag needs a bone along either side of its opening and very often in the body of the bag as well to keep its shape (Fig. 139).

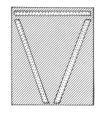

Fig. 139. Boning on the side of the tote bag

60 Denim tote bag with webbing handle and gussets made in one piece. Decorated with machine fixed embroidery stitches and machine quilted on to a foam rubber interlining. $13\frac{1}{2}$ in × $15\frac{1}{2}$ in (34 cm × 38 cm)

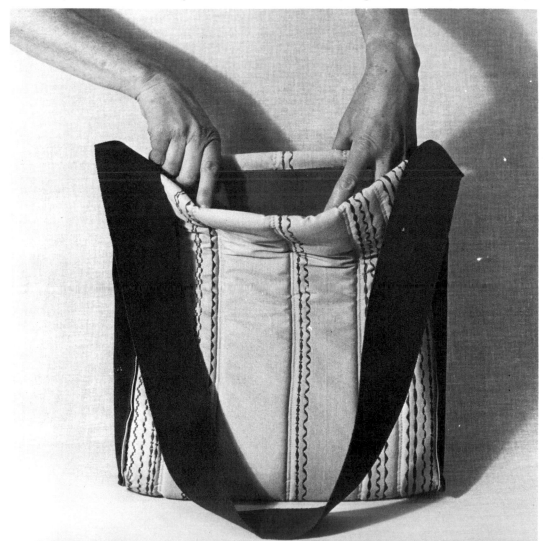

TO MAKE UP The body of the bag can be top-stitched to the gusset from the outside (Fig. 140), or seamed from the inside in the normal way.

The lining can be cut to cover the whole of the inside of the bag, or just the body of the bag if webbing is being used.

A stiff base can be inserted into the lining, so that it folds up parallel to the bag sides and allows the bag to collapse flat (see LININGS AND FITTINGS, page 124).

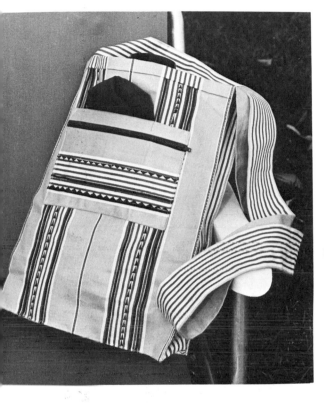

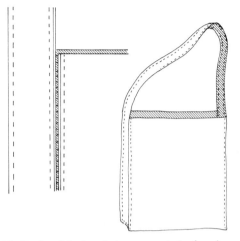

Fig. 140. Body of the bag being top-stitched to the gusset from the outside

61 Red ticking tote bag with machine-fixed embroidery stitching. The long handle is made in one piece with the gussets and base and is top-stitched into position. 11½ in × 15½ in (29 cm × 38 cm)

Gussets Cut in One Piece with the Base and the Handle (Plate 61)

This type is very similar to the previous style, but this time the handle is taken all the way round the sides and base with the body of the bag inserted on either side. The methods of handling are the same.

Plate 61 shows an example in ticking, with sides cut double in length so that it is self-lined. Each side is stitched and turned out and then top-stitched to the handle. The handle piece being already stitched double and pulled through to the right side is therefore lined and neatened. No interlining need be used as ticking has plenty of body.

A tuck should be made on the top edge to mask the abrupt finish of the machine-fixed embroidery patterns and to give a good neat edge.

A bag of this style could, of course, have an independent lining and a zip or flap.

Linings and Fittings

All linings should have a calico interlining. The weight of the calico required depends on the size of the bag and how much strain will be put on the lining by the fittings.

Any of the following types of pockets can be used on the inside or outside of the bag. The construction will be the same; only the fabric will vary.

Flat Pocket

A piece of fabric is cut twice the height required for the pocket plus turnings and a piece of interlining the size of the pocket plus turnings. Lay the two together on the wrong side and tack round (Fig. 141). Fold the fabric in half on the edge of the interlining, right sides to right sides. Stitch round leaving a gap at the bottom, press and turn through to the right side. The fold is the top edge of the pocket and the unstitched section at the bottom will be secured when the pocket is top-stitched into position. It is always worth working a buttonhole bar over the edge of the pocket onto the lining to help the wear and tear (Fig. 141d).

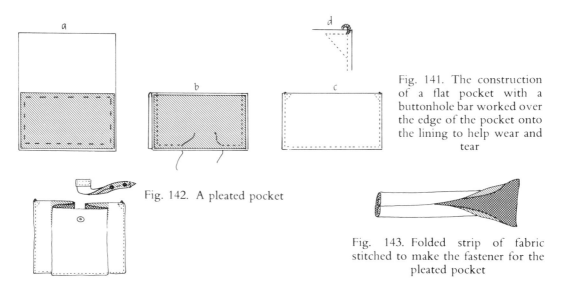

Fig. 141. The construction of a flat pocket with a buttonhole bar worked over the edge of the pocket onto the lining to help wear and tear

Fig. 142. A pleated pocket

Fig. 143. Folded strip of fabric stitched to make the fastener for the pleated pocket

Pleated Pocket

Made as a flat pocket this has a box pleat to give extra space and a fastener (Fig. 142).

The fastener is a folded strip of fabric (Fig. 143), either stitched on the inside and pulled through, or folded over to conceal the raw edges and top stitched. One end is attached to the lining and the other end has two press stud heads on it, to fit the one stud base which is sewn onto the centre of the pocket. One head is used to keep the pocket flat against the lining when it is not being used and the other one holds the pocket firm when it is full.

Work a buttonhole bar between the lining and the pocket on the seam line to strengthen the stitching.

Inserted Zipped Pocket (Plate 50, page 109)
A bound buttonhole is made (Fig. 144) and a zip inserted. A calico pocket is sewn onto the back (Fig. 145).

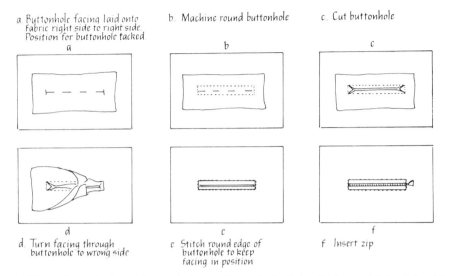

Fig. 144. Making a bound, zipped buttonhole a. Buttonhole facing laid onto fabric right side to right side. Position for buttonhole tacked. b. Machine round buttonhole. c. Cut buttonhole. d. Turn facing through buttonhole to wrong side. e. Stitch round edge of buttonhole to keep facing in position. f. Insert zip

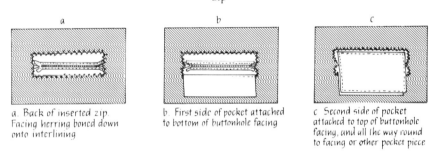

Fig. 145. Attaching a pocket to the back a. Back of inserted zip. Facing herringboned down onto interlining. b. First side of pocket attached to bottom of buttonhole facing. c. Second side of pocket attached to top of buttonhole facing, and all the way round to facing or other pocket piece

Zipped Pocket (Plate 61)
Cut two pieces of fabric the size of the required pocket, plus turnings. Lay interlining as required onto the wrong side of both pieces. Insert a zip between the two long edges (Fig. 146).

Fold the pocket into position right sides to right sides and stitch round (Fig. 147). Press. Undo the zip and turn the pocket to the right side. Press.

Make a lining in a similar way and drop into the pocket. Hem the top edges to the tape of the zip. Be careful not to set the lining too close to the zip or it will get caught up during use.

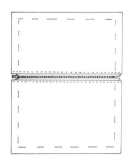

Fig. 146. A zip inserted between the
two sections of pocket

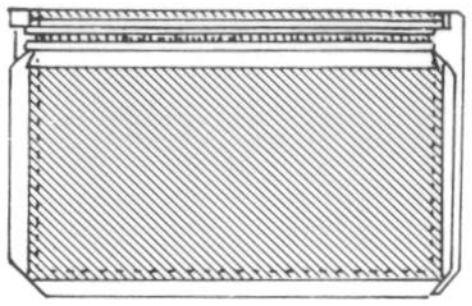

Fig. 147. Pocket folded into position,
right sides to right sides and machined
up

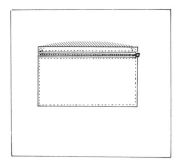

Fig. 148. Zipped pocket machined
into position, giving a pocket behind
it as well

Fig. 149. A card base covered with
lining fabric ready for inserting into
the lining base seam

The 'purse' type pocket can now be top-stitched into position (Fig. 148). As well as a zipped pocket, this gives a pocket between itself and the main fabric. Work a buttonhole bar between the lining and the pocket on the seam line to strengthen the stitching.

Pockets can be tailored to any size to fit personal accessories like compacts, lipstick, glasses, tickets, etc.

Stiffened Base Attached to Lining

A piece of thick card $\frac{1}{4}$ in (5 mm) smaller in both directions than the main lining is enclosed in a fitted bag made of the lining fabric and interlining (Fig. 149). The turnings are left jutting outwards on one long side.

The main lining is cut in the normal way, with the gussets and base cut in one piece or separately. Before stitching together, the turnings of the covered base card are inserted into the lining base seam. Stitch and press.

This loose base can be pushed flat in the bottom of the bag for use, or can be lifted to allow the bag to be packed flat.

Attaching Metal-Frame Tops

The traditional metal frames (Fig. 150) need a shaped gusset to fit round the sides of the frame (Fig. 151).

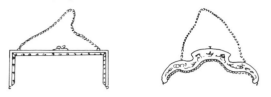

Fig. 150. Metal frames

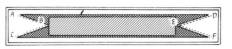

Fig. 151. Shaped gusset to fit round a metal frame

Side Gussets and Base in One Piece

One edge of the gusset 'V' shape fits on the front of the metal frame (Fig. 152) C B, and the other edge fits on the back of the frame A B. Similarly for other end F E and D E.

Calico is laid onto the shape of the gusset and an additional Vilene interlining used between B and E to stiffen the sides and base of the bag if required.

The lines of the 'V' shapes are machined to strengthen the edge and to prevent stretching and fraying.

The long edges A D and C F of the gusset are stitched onto the back and front pieces of the bag, the seams trimmed and pressed.

The 'V' A B C is cut with turnings and herringboned back onto the wrong side. Similarly the 'V' D E F.

The turnings on the top edges of the bag A D and C F are also herringboned back onto the wrong side.

Make up the lining to the same pattern and slip it inside the bag, wrong sides to wrong sides. Turn the raw edges in and pin the lining to the edge of the bag, matching points A, B, C, D, E and F. Ladder-stitch the edges together.

Oversew the metal frame onto the bag as a form of tacking in order to hold it in position whilst sewing the bag to the frame (Fig. 153).

There are two methods of sewing the bag to the frame and the choice very much depends on the character of the bag and what it is made of.

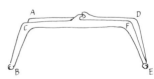

Fig. 152. Relative points on the metal frame to the shaped gusset for attaching

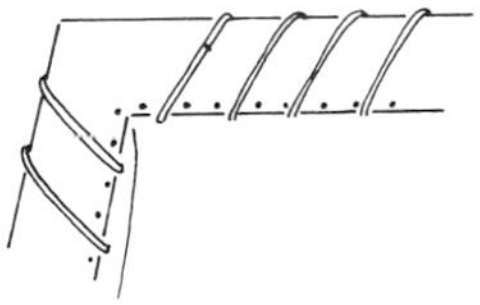

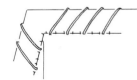

Fig. 153. The bag and frame tacked together with oversewing

Fig. 154. The bag oversewn onto the frame, having been tacked first

METHOD 1 (Fig. 154) The frame is oversewn into position, the thread passing from the bag into a hole in the metal frame with a stitch at right angles to the edge (Fig. 154). This is the shortest possible stitch to make and therefore will show the least.

Sloping or thonging stitches can be used on a larger edition of the handle in wood or tortoiseshell, if it suits the character of the article (Fig. 155).

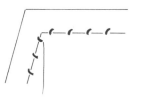

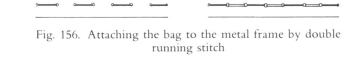

Fig. 156. Attaching the bag to the metal frame by double running stitch

Fig. 155. Decorative thonging to attach the bag to the metal frame

METHOD 2 This is a very neat method, using double running-stitch through the holes in the frame into the edge of the bag. A running or stab-stitch is made through the holes for the full length of the frame and then repeated in the opposite direction. This time the stitch is made in the gaps of the first row, so that it has the appearance of a back-stitch on both sides of the work (Fig. 156).

If no extra width is required at the base of the bag, the gusset pattern can be adjusted to make side gussets only. The methods for attaching the bag to the frame remain the same.

If the top-stitching on the frame is unacceptable to the design, a tiny matching gimp can be glued on top of the stitching. Be very careful to choose a small one, as otherwise it can be very clumsy.

Having appreciated the basic constructional shapes of these bags, many designs can be evolved, in any size.

It is well worth while spraying the finished article with a soil-resistant fabric protector, but do test on an off-cut of the fabric first, to make sure that it does not leave any stains.

CHAPTER FOUR

Cushions

Designing the Cushion

Cushions can play a vital part in the decoration schemes of our homes. Being small, and taking comparatively so much less material than the other soft furnishings they are replaceable at more frequent intervals, and can lay emphasis on a different colour that is a part of the general scheme. This can give a completely new look to a room.

In a single colour scheme, which is frequently used in a bedroom, a pile of cushions made up in a variety of tone values can give a lift and add interest to the whole room (Plate 62).

62 Small print used to decorate a co-ordinating set of patchwork cushions. *Sara Getley*

In the same way in a gentle colour scheme a couple of cushions in a sharp contrast can give the bite and accent that the room had previously lacked.

Larger cushions are the most comfortable, but it is the smaller ones of various shapes that can be the most interesting in the way that they are used. Some of them have a continuing theme that takes four or five cushions to cover, one side of the cushions showing the front of the motif and the reverse showing the back of the motif. A reclining figure is one obvious example of this sort of design. Other cushions have a strong geometric design, varying on several cushions, but all fitting together whichever way they are laid.

The important thing to remember when designing a cushion, or set of cushions, is that each one must be complete in itself, complement the others, and have a design that is satisfactory when viewed from all directions.

Canvas-work, patchwork and quilting are widely used techniques for cushions. They wear well and do not get distorted with use. Free stitchery can make lovely cushion covers, but care must be taken to keep the stitches short so that there are no long threads to get caught in fingers, buttons or animal claws!

Tools and Materials

Fabric for Cover
This needs to fit into the colour scheme and to have the right textured quality for its position. It also needs to be strong enough for the amount of wear that it is going to receive. For instance, a cushion for the garden or playroom is going to have to stand up to much harder wear than one that decorates a bedroom chair.

When the fabric is being chosen it should be considered whether it is essential or not for the cover to be washable. Many man-made fibres are drip-dry, but they are not always sympathetic to embroidery techniques. Natural fibres are so much nicer to handle. Many of these can be carefully washed, but where several fabrics are used together, it is safer to have the cover dry cleaned in case each reacts differently when put in water.

Trimmings
These vary with fashion from frills and fringes to piping or nothing at all. Personally I like piping as it gives a good crisp finish and helps to retain the cushion's shape.

Sewing Machine
Although cushions can be made entirely by hand a machine does take a lot of the grind out of the job and is obviously much quicker. A piping foot is essential when inserting piping by machine.

Normal Sewing Equipment
Scissors, needles, pins, tape measure, tailor's chalk, suitable thread to match the fabric, and tacking cotton.

Cushion Pads

Fillings

DOWN This is the soft underfeathers of birds, the eider-duck providing the finest quality down of all. Unfortunately all down is expensive but it does provide an excellent filling, being soft, resilient and holding its shape for years. It is well worth while using the filling from an old eiderdown to make a set of cushions, especially if they are to be made of silk.

The best place to handle loose feathers or filling of any sort, is in the bath. Shut all the windows and doors so that there are no draughts, and wear cotton or something that the feathers will not stick to. Otherwise it takes longer to tidy up than it does to fill the cushion pads!

DOWN AND FEATHER This is a cheaper mixture and makes very good cushions. Feathers on their own can be rather heavy, but they are perfectly satisfactory for larger cushions made in a tough furnishing fabric.

KAPOK This silky vegetable fibre is light in weight and relatively inexpensive. A disadvantage is a tendency to go lumpy, but as it does not absorb moisture it can be acceptable for garden cushions.

MAN-MADE FIBRES Courtelle, Dacron and Terylene and similar waddings are inexpensive, non-absorbent, and washable. They give a firm cushion, but cannot be compared to down, or down and feather for that bouncy quality that looks so inviting with a good cushion.

LATEX AND PLASTIC FOAM Obtainable in various shapes and sizes, and from $\frac{1}{8}$ in (3 mm) to 4 in (10 cm) in thickness, the sheets can easily be cut to size with a sharp carving knife. They both make good tailored seat pads or cushions, but Latex is the firmest, and so will retain its shape longest. Both types require a thin calico inner cover to close fit the pad, otherwise it sticks to the cushion cover and does not look tidy.

PLASTIC FOAM CHIPS An inexpensive filling which gives a very lumpy finish that spoils the appearance of any cushion.

POLYSTYRENE BEADS These are excellent for large floor cushions as they mould round the body, yet give firm support. They also reflect body heat so are warm to use. They are, however, totally unsuitable for small cushions for if the pad is filled completely it is hard and unyielding, and if only partially filled the beads fall to the bottom of the inner cover and the cushion cannot retain its shape.

OLD NYLON STOCKINGS AND TIGHTS Cut up into small bits these can be used for filling a pad, but a great deal are needed to fill a cushion.

Inner Covers
The choice of fabric to cover the pad depends on the filling that is being used.

DOWN-PROOF CAMBRIC This has a specially prepared surface to prevent the down working through. A double row of machine stitching on the seams is required when making up the inner cover. The seams should be rubbed with beeswax or a candle to seal off the needle holes.

FEATHER-PROOF TICKING A heavier fabric than the down-proof cambric, it is handled in the same way. It is available in plain white, but should a traditional striped one be used, do check that the stripe does not show through the top cushion cover fabric.

CALICO Bleached or un-bleached, this is suitable for all inner covers other than with down or feather fillings. Remnants of curtain lining and the good corners of worn out sheets are also suitable.

To Make the Pad
LOOSE FILLING To make sure that the finished cushion has a well filled appearance, the inner pad needs to be 1 in (3 cm) larger all round than the outer cushion cover. This means that an 18-in (46-cm) square cushion needs a pad measuring 20 in (51 cm) square.

PLASTIC FOAM PADS These have quite a lot of 'give' in them, but not as much as the loose fillings, so the pad is only $\frac{1}{2}$ in (15 mm) larger all round than the outer cushion cover. This means that an 18-in (46-cm) square cushion needs a pad 19 in (48 cm) square. If the foam pad is 3 in (17 cm) deep then the side band needs to be made 2 in (5 cm) wide.

LATEX FOAM PADS The pads should be cut to the exact size of the outer cushion cover as they have a much closer texture and are consequently much firmer.

Piping

Piping cord is available in many sizes and the finished piping must be nicely in proportion to the cushion. Do not forget that a thick fabric will increase the width of the piping cord by quite a lot, so that a narrower one is needed than thought by first impressions.

Piping cord should always be washed and brought to the boil before covering, as it shrinks and could easily spoil a cushion the first time that it is washed.

Piping Cut on the Cross Grain
Piping cord is covered with a crossway strip of fabric. For the normal range of cords used, a $1\frac{1}{2}$-in (4-cm) width is all that is required to allow for the two turnings and the

centre piece which covers the cord (Fig. 157). For the very heavy cords more width is needed.

The strips of fabric must be joined on the straight grain; this gives a seam on the diagonal (Fig. 158).

The piping is prepared for use by folding the fabric round the cord with the edges together, and tacking a line close to the cord (Fig. 159).

If a lot of piping is going to be needed it is much quicker to cut a piping sleeve. Cut a wide piece of crossway fabric (Fig. 160). Fold it in half so that the short edges lie together, but with one width of a piping strip jutting out at each side (Fig. 161). Stitch the seam and press it open.

Start cutting a width of crossway from the single jutting out piece, and continue cutting round and round the sleeve until the other end is reached (Fig. 162).

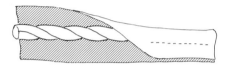

Fig. 157. A bias strip covering the piping cord

Fig. 158. Joining two strips of fabric cut on the cross grain

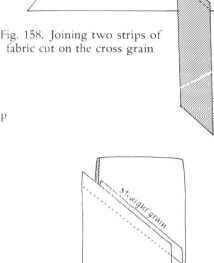

Fig. 159. Tacking the bias strip round the piping cord

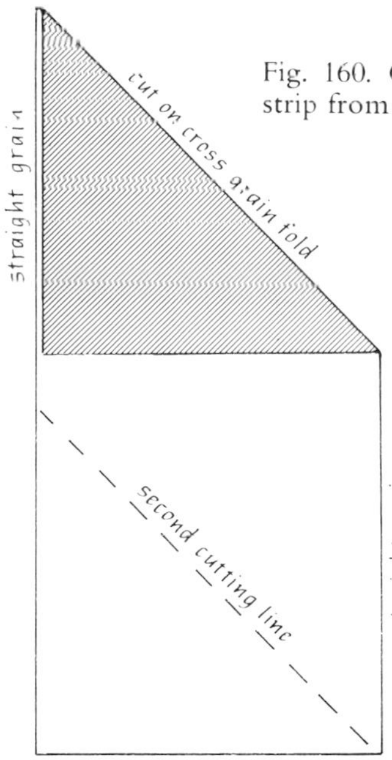

Fig. 160. Cutting a wide bias strip from a length of material

Fig. 161. The bias strip prepared for cutting

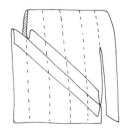

Fig. 162. Cutting the piping sleeve

Piping Cut on Straight Grain

For tailored, box-sided cushions (Fig. 163) it is possible to lay piping cord into the two long edges of the side band. The band is cut on the straight grain, long enough to go right round the cushion. Piping is then tacked into the edges, before machining on the top and bottom pieces (Fig. 164). Although the edge does not have quite the crispness of a biased-covered piping being laid in separately, it is perfectly acceptable, and only discernible on close inspection. It can certainly be the answer where fabric is short, and a contrasting coloured piping is not called for.

The results are not so good on a striped fabric, unless very carefully placed. The crossway piping is a much better finish. If fabric were short a contrasting coloured piping to pick up one of the stripes could well be used.

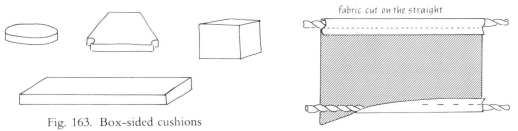

Fig. 163. Box-sided cushions

Fig. 164. Piping set into the straight side bands

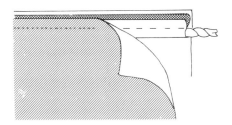

Fig. 165. Inserting the piping

Inserting the Piping

The back and front pieces of the cushion cover are laid right side to right side, and the piping inserted between them with the piping turnings lying edge to edge with the cushion turnings (Fig. 165).

Joining the Piping

The piping join should be made one third of the way along the side where the opening will be made for the insertion of the pad. This is so that the least tidy side of the cushion can be laid to the back, or to the bottom as the case may be, when the cushion is in position.

Never attempt a piping join on the corner of the cushion, as it will be difficult to achieve a neat result.

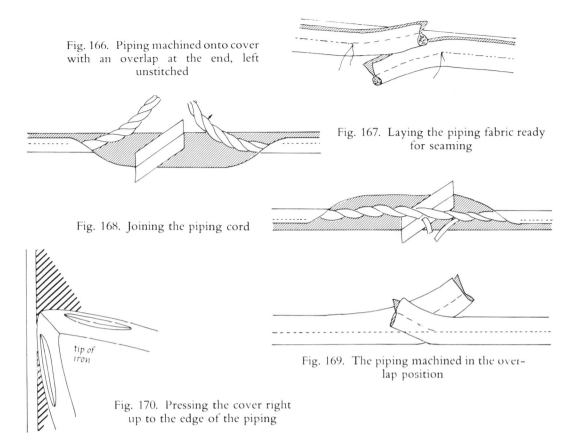

Fig. 166. Piping machined onto cover with an overlap at the end, left unstitched

Fig. 167. Laying the piping fabric ready for seaming

Fig. 168. Joining the piping cord

Fig. 169. The piping machined in the overlap position

Fig. 170. Pressing the cover right up to the edge of the piping

tip of iron

METHOD 1 Tack the piping into position and machine as closely as possible to the cord, leaving 1 in (3 cm) overlapping either end unstitched (Fig. 166).

Open back the piping and trim the fabric so that it will make a seam on the straight grain with $\frac{3}{8}$-in (10-mm) turnings (Fig. 167).

Cut the two ends of the piping cord so that there is 1 in (3 cm) overlap.

Unravel the two ends and cut half the thickness of cord away on each end for the last inch (3 cm) (Fig. 168).

Wind the two ends together so that they lie correctly on the stitching line, fold the fabric back into place, and stitch the 2 in (5 cm) of piping to the cover.

Ladder-stitch the seam in the piping.

METHOD 2 The piping is tacked into position on the cover with 1 in (3 cm) overlap on each end.

The cord is cut back inside the fabric so that it exactly meets.

The piping is then machined in the overlap position (Fig. 169).

Press the seam from the inside with the turnings together, then on the outside right up to the piping (Fig. 170), using a damp cloth if necessary. This makes the piping stand up sharply.

Fastenings

Fashions and theories have changed with the years. At one time it was thought essential to work an elaborate opening in the middle of the back of the cover with hand-made buttons as part of the decoration. Later 'invisible' plackets were made in the seam with hooks and eyes, and press studs.

The small nylon zip is a satisfactory method and it comes in a wide range of colours; but now with the very high cost of zips, which are never really invisible and do add bulk, I personally think that the best finish is to ladder-stitch the seam together. It is quickly unpicked for cleaning and only takes a few minutes to re-stitch afterwards.

Order of Work

This list is intended to help in the making of cushions, but please check points in later paragraphs before embarking on them.

1. Plan colour of cushion or set of cushions.
2. Choose fabric and design treatment.
3. Make or buy the pad. Check size of pad if it is already available.
4. Remember that:
    Soft-filled pads need to be 2 in (5 cm) bigger than the cover.
    Foam-rubber pads need to be 1 in (3 cm) bigger than the cover.
    Latex rubber pads need to be the same size as the cover.
5. Cut the cover as a rectangle or square whatever the shape of the embroidery and block before trimming the fabric to the required shape for the cushion.
6. Plan the trimming. Make the piping if required.
7. Make up cover. Insert ties if required for chair pads.
8. Trim.
9. Insert pad.
10. Ladder-stitch opening together, or insert a zip if preferred.

Standard Cushions (Plate 63)

A well-filled square or rectangular cushion is distorted in shape and appears to have a waist (Fig. 171). This can be rectified by curving each seam outwards, about 1 in (3 cm) depending on the size of the cushion (Fig. 172).

This cannot be done if the curved line would show up badly against the straight grain of the fabric. For example where the top of the cushion is canvas-work or patchwork it would be very obvious and unacceptable.

Having measured the pad, or made it to the required size it is possible to cut the cover, adding turnings all the way round of $\frac{1}{2}$ in–$\frac{3}{4}$ in (1 cm–2 cm). The amount of turnings allowed vary according to the fabric and the amount that it frays.

Plan to have either square corners or rounded corners, and make sure that they all match.

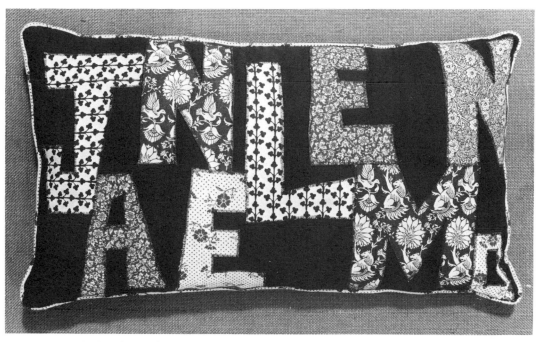

63 Letters applied with Bondaweb and a zig-zag machine stitch, to spell out a name on one side of the cushion. 21 in × 12 in (54 cm × 31 cm). *Designed by Jane Lemon, made by Sara Getley*

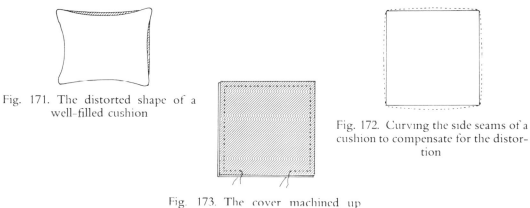

Fig. 171. The distorted shape of a well-filled cushion

Fig. 172. Curving the side seams of a cushion to compensate for the distortion

Fig. 173. The cover machined up leaving a section open

To Make Up

Tack in the piping if it is being used and machine round leaving a section open on one side for inserting the pad (Fig. 173). The piping must be machined to the front of the cover in the opening. Machine round a second time and trim the turnings back close to the second row. If the fabric is thick it is better to layer the seam to avoid bulk (Fig. 174). This can then be oversewn or zig-zagged by machine (Fig. 175).

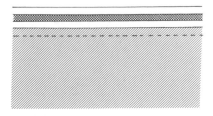
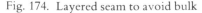

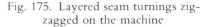

Fig. 174. Layered seam to avoid bulk

Fig. 175. Layered seam turnings zig-zagged on the machine

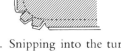

Fig. 176. Snipping into the turnings of a square corner

Fig. 177. Snipping into the turnings of a rounded corner

Fig. 178. Ties inserted into the piping seam on the underside of the cushion

Snip into the turnings at the corners so that the cover turns through to the right side cleanly (Figs 176 and 177). If there are still puckers check the machine to make sure that the tension is correct and not too tight.

Some trimmings need to be laid into the seams, and these are machined into position like the piping, others are laid on top when the cover is complete. The latter should have their ends turned under and be butted together. Others may need whipping together on the wrong side as neatly as possible.

Tailored Box-Sided Cushions (Plate 64)

These box-sided cushions have a strip round them to allow for the depth of the pad and are usually piped.

If the pad is made of foam rubber the depth of the band is made up 1 in (3 cm) less than the depth of the foam. If latex rubber is used then the band is made to the same depth as the latex.

These cushions are often used for squab seats so may need ties to keep them in position. These are best made of folds of the same fabric, but if the material is very thick matching coloured tape should be used.

This type of cushion sits best if it is tied to the four legs of the chair, rather than to the back. The ties should be inserted into the lower seam of the cushion on either side of the corner (Fig. 178).

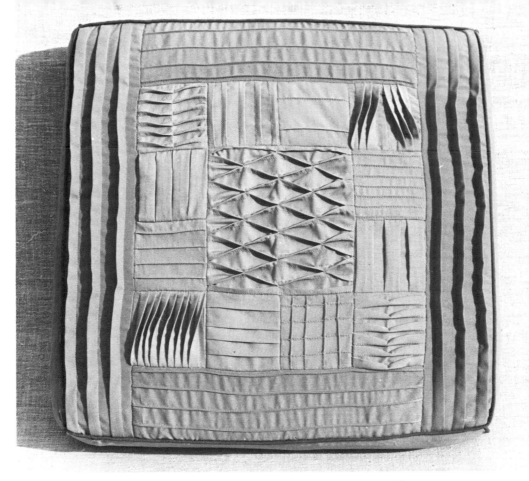

64 Pleated and tucked tailored cushion in terylene cotton. 12 in × 12 in × 2½ in (30 cm × 30 cm × 6 cm).
Diane Keay

Fig. 179. An opening left in the back
seam with the piping attached

To Make Up
The strip of fabric for the side band, with piping if required, is tacked round the
underside of the cover, right side of fabric to right side of fabric.

The join in the side strip can then be positioned, tacked, seamed and pressed before
machining the band and cover together. Leave an opening on the back seam, just
machining the piping into position if it is loose (Fig. 179). If the piping is made in one
with the side band it is only necessary to leave part of the back seam unstitched.

With the wrong sides outside, pin and tack the top of the cover into position and
machine. Finish as for standard cushions.

Canvas-work makes a very suitable top to a tailored cushion, and tweed, furnishing velvet, or a number of other heavy fabrics can marry very happily with it for the rest of the cushion (Plates 65 and 66).

The side band is cut ¼ in (5 mm) deeper to allow for this finish. The base, side band, and piping for the lower edge is cut in the fabric, and made up in the usual way.

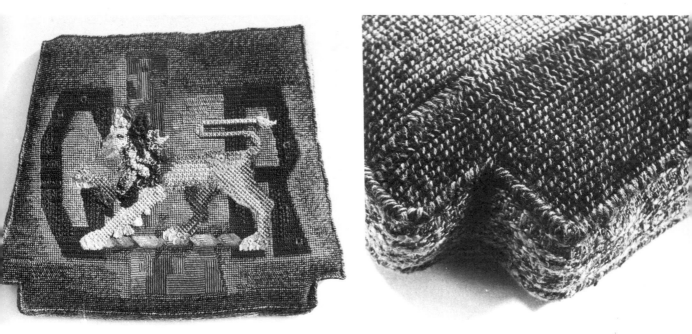

65 Canvas chair pad mounted on tweed sides and back, made for a Charles II carver. 21 in × 17 in × 1½ in (53 cm × 43 cm × 4 cm)

66 Detail showing the simulated piping that joins the canvas and tweed

The join between the canvas and the fabric is then worked as follows:

Having worked the canvas, block it and trim to 1-in (3-cm) turnings. Paint the raw edges of the canvas with rubber solution to prevent fraying. Allow to dry thoroughly.

Turn the seam allowance over to the back of the work leaving two unworked rows of canvas on the right side.

On any curved edge, like a round corner, a gathering thread should be laid round the turnings on the wrong side to help them to lie flat with the fullness evenly distributed.

Herringbone the turning to the back of the worked canvas to keep it flat.

The turnings on the top edge of the side band are folded over and tacked. The two folded edges of the canvas and the side band are then laid edge to edge (Fig. 180) wrong side to wrong side, in the correct position for the corners to line up, and a form of long armed cross-stitch is worked over the four thicknesses of materials to simulate a piped finish in wool (Fig. 181).

67 Patchwork cylindrical cushion in shaded pinks and purples. 18 in × 8 in (46 cm × 20 cm).
Diane Browne

Fig. 180. The folded edges of the canvas and the side band laid together with the long armed cross stitch being worked

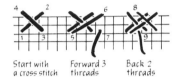

Fig. 181. Plaited edging stitch to simulate a piped finish

Cylindrical Cushions (Plate 67)

These can be very useful in a bed–sitting room as they can help transform a divan bed into a sofa by forming armrests. The cover can be made to size to take a rolled up pillow as its pad, which answers a storage problem. A long cushion can be made to run the length of the bed, which gives support to the other cushions, and is padded with a rolled eiderdown when not in use. As long as they are made especially to fit the required 'pad' or stuffing they work extremely well.

Obviously for something of this nature zips are essential for the placket, and for the long cushion two zips are needed opening from the centre outwards to within 3 or 4 in (7 or 10 cm) of the ends.

A cylindrical cushion is made of a rectangle and two circular end pieces (Fig. 182). To work out the diameter of the circular ends, to a given circumference of the circle, use the following formula.

Diameter of a circle = circumference ÷ 3·142

or

Circumference of a circle = diameter × 3·142

So, if the length of the rectangle which is going to stitch onto the circumference of the two end circles is 16, *the diameter* of each circle is 16 ÷ 3·142 = 5·09.

Therefore the *radius* used to draw the circle with a compass is 5·09 ÷ 2 = 2·54.

To Make Up

With wrong sides outside, pin the short ends of the rectangle round the circular ends, keeping the edges of the turnings together. When it is pinned smoothly round, the long seams can be positioned, seamed and pressed, leaving a placket open.

Tack the seam round the circular ends, machine, trim and press.

If the cushion is to have a permanent pad the opening can be in one of the circular ends, which can be ladder-stitched up when the pad has been positioned inside.

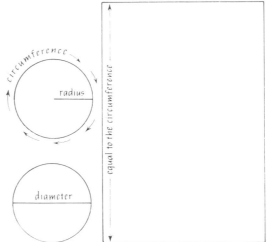

Fig. 182. Pattern for a cylindrical cushion

68 One long strip embroidered and joined up to form tetrahedrons. The cushion turns inside out to reveal different designs. The length of each side of the triangles is 5 in (13 cm).

Variegated Shaped Cushions

Cushions can come in all shapes and sizes (Plate 68), and as long as the basic principles are followed there should not be any problems.

The important thing is to snip into the seams to make sure that the various curves and angles lie neatly without any awkward wrinkles and puckers.

Always press the seams on the wrong side before turning the cover through to the right side. Make sure you put enough filling into the pad, and use a small ladder-stitch for sewing up the opening.

CHAPTER FIVE

Curtains

Designing the Curtains

Before thinking about the actual embroidery it is vital to decide on the size of the curtains and their relationship to the window and the rest of the room. Curtains can do a great deal to improve the proportions of the window and the room in general.

To give a much greater feeling of width, and to avoid losing any of the light, curtains should be hung from a rail that runs above the top of the window and then extends 18–24 in (46–61 cm) along the wall on either side. This means that the curtains will lie against the wall when drawn back and not obscure any of the window.

Floor-length curtains nearly always improve a wall, but cannot be used if they block out a window seat or radiator. But care must be taken as to the length of the curtains above this point, so that they do not cut the wall in half but give a good proportion with their block of colour against the wall.

In cottages which have rooms with low ceilings and small windows, light and wall space are at a premium. In these old buildings the walls are nearly always very thick and use can be made of this depth to great advantage. The rail is placed on the window frame within the thickness of the wall, and then curved round the depth of the wall at the sides to the near edge. At night the curtains hang in an attractive curve still allowing the use of the deep windowsills, whilst in the daytime they hang against the thickness of the wall, neither robbing daylight nor using the wall space within the room itself.

High rooms often need a pelmet to shorten the elongated height of the windows, and they can look extremely elegant, but in many modern rooms a pelmet of any sort merely cuts across the line of the curtains and makes it look lower than it is. Curtains with ornamental pleated heads hung from camouflaged rods or poles of various types, usually look best in these rooms.

If a wall has two or three individual windows within a small area it is well worth while considering whether the whole wall would be improved by curtaining it completely, rather than by breaking it up with individual blocks of curtain.

Bearing in mind the problems of squat shallow windows or tall narrow ones, it will be appreciated how embroidery designs can counteract or exaggerate a problem. A stripe or border in the wrong direction is no asset to the decoration.

Embroidery on curtains should help the proportions and add to the general decorative scheme. It is important that it is in the right scale for the size of the curtains and the room. This does not mean that large stitches are needed, but that the design is strong enough 'to read' from the other side of the room, and yet to blend with the other patterns.

It is also important to design a motif or pattern that looks right when it is hanging in folds, because that will be its normal position.

Café curtains are the exception to this rule, as if they have a decorative heading they need to hang flat.

Curtains fall into five main groups.

Sheer Curtains

These allow the light to pass through but obscure the vision so that people are prevented from seeing in from the road, or an unattractive view is camouflaged from the room. They can also form room dividers.

The techniques especially suited to this group are drawn thread stitches worked on the warp and weft of the fabric without withdrawing any more threads; pulled work on the very loosely woven wools or linens; shadow work and net darning.

Unlined Curtains

These are only really suitable for the bathroom or kitchen where the humid atmosphere would make thicker curtains permanently damp, and readily absorbent to cooking smells.

Lined Curtains

Tweed and heavy velvet have enough substance in themselves to make excellent curtains with just ordinary curtain lining.

A lining gives a good finish to a curtain and definitely improves the way that it hangs or drapes.

A detachable lining may seem to have its advantages since, being made up separately, it is easily removed for washing or cleaning, but it does not do its job as well as the permanent lining.

Interlined Curtains

For all except very heavy fabrics, interlining gives an added richness and quality that makes all the difference to curtains. It makes any fabric hang better with stronger folds and the cheaper fabrics certainly improve out of all recognition. Interlining also acts as insulation against cold and noise.

In my opinion it should always be used, with a few obvious exceptions such as the café curtains described below and those already mentioned.

Café Curtains

These curtains, which cover the lower third of the window (half is an unhappy proportion), are suspended from a decorative pole and remain in position all the time (Fig. 183). They camouflage the lower part of the view, but leave the tree tops and sky in full vision.

Curtains to hang on the two thirds of the window for drawing at night can certainly be made, but in fact café curtains combine very much better with a blind, a pair of full-length curtains drawn in front of them, or louvred shutters on the inside wall.

The main feature of café curtains is a decorative heading, and if one is used the curtains need to hang flat in order to show the heading to advantage. This in turn gives much more scope for the embroidery design.

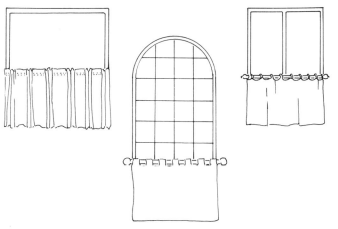

Fig. 183. Café curtains

Tools and Materials

Fabric

The colour and patterns of a fabric for curtains needs to be looked at hanging up, as it will have quite a different appearance lying flat on a counter. The colour should also be seen by daylight as well as artificial light as it can change disastrously.

Do check that the fabric is guaranteed against fading; otherwise the sun can fade it very quickly, especially in the case of unlined curtains.

Enquire whether the fabric has to be dry cleaned or can be washed. If the latter, make sure that it is shrink resistant. As all curtains with interlinings have to be cleaned, this is not always such a necessary factor.

Lining

Not only does a lining help the curtains to hang better, but it protects the fibres of the main fabric from dust as well as the extremes of sunlight and frost which will make them rot.

It is well worth while using the recommended lining sateens, as a cheaper fabric will wear out before the curtains and they will need remaking.

Cotton sateen is available in a wide range of colours which can be bought to match the curtains, but do make sure that a coloured lining does not alter the colour of the fabric by daylight. If the curtains are to be interlined there should be no colour change, as the light should not penetrate through to the main fabric.

There is a lining sateen that is treated with a silver metallic finish for the purpose of aiding insulation.

Interlinings
BUMP A thick soft material made from cotton waste, it is made in curtain fabric width and is available bleached or unbleached.

DOMETTE This is a similar type of fabric but has less body.

FLANNELETTE SHEETING This is a suitable substitute and does very well on smaller curtains, but it does not have the body of bump.

Wadding
COURTELLE OR TERYLENE Sheet wadding made from synthetic fibres is used for quilted borders or padded hems and gives a luxurious finish.

Vilene or Pellon
IRON-ON VILENE OR BONDAWEB These fuse two fabrics together and are both useful for applied designs and motifs. They prevent fraying whilst the edges are being treated.

LIGHT-WEIGHT VILENE This may be useful for interlining borders before mounting them onto the curtains. It depends on the finished look that is required.

MEDIUM-WEIGHT VILENE Used as interlining, this gives extra body to scalloped or castellated headings for café curtains.

PELMET VILENE A heavy-weight interlining, this can be used as an alternative to buckram when making pelmets.

BUCKRAM This stiffened fabric can be obtained in a special weight for making pelmets.

Weights
Lead weights inserted into tape at regular intervals can be bought by the length. This is laid into hems to give the additional weight necessary for some curtains to hang with stronger folds.

Tools

SCISSORS Good cutting-out shears and smaller sewing scissors are vital.

PINS Glass-headed pins are useful on sheers; the long fine ones are the nicest to use on other curtains.

MEASURING TOOLS A metre or yard rule in wood or metal is more accurate than a tape measure for long measurements. A tape measure with a stiff end is also helpful. It is worth making your own card measures (Fig. 184) for checking hem and heading depths.

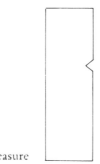

Fig. 184. Card measure

THREAD Use matching coloured thread to the fabric. Man-made fibres are the easiest to use. It is advisable to use tacking cotton rather than left-over reels.

NEEDLES These need to suit the fabric. Sharps and Betweens 7–9 should fulfil most general needs.

TAILOR'S CHALK This is a useful marker which is easily removed.

'QUICK UNPICK' This small tool used for unpicking stitches is a great time-saver.

SEWING MACHINE Although a machine is invaluable for doing some of the long seams and some headings, the best results are achieved by laying in the interlining and lining by hand.

IRON AND IRONING BOARD It is always important to press each seam as it is worked. The same crisp result is never achieved if the pressing is all done at the end. With experience, pressing can save a lot of time and tacking as all the headings and hems can be prepared by measuring, pressing and pinning on the ironing board.

Note Where an interlining or a padded edge is being used the sides and hems look better left with a rolled edge and not a pressed crease.

Borders

These are a very attractive addition to a pair of curtains, and look at their best when used on interlined curtains.

COARSE LACE Lace can be used on curtains with a tiny pattern as well as on plain fabrics.

DIFFERENT WIDTH RIBBONS These can be laid one on top of another to form a clean-cut decoration (Plate 69). This particular example has threaded herringbone stitch running up the middle using a weaving thread to slide through the herringbone stitch.

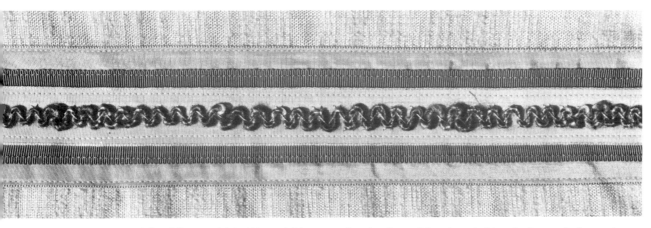

69 Three different width ribbons laid on top of each other, with a threaded herringbone stitch running up the middle to make a curtain border. 2¼ in (5½ cm) wide

QUILTING This is a very lively technique showing up the light and shade in a fabric. Plate 70 shows a corner section of a border worked on a silky fabric with a slub weave.

A quilted border may need a little stiffening and control before applying onto the curtain, in which case it should be interlined with a light-weight Vilene, and the turnings herringboned back onto the Vilene before applying the border with ladder-stitch on both edges.

PRINTED BORDERS These can be cut from ordinary curtain fabric and laid onto the curtain (Plate 75, page 161). The long seam nearest the edge is machined on first on the wrong side of the border, then it is folded over, pressed, and the second edge prepared for ladder-stitching into place. This border could well have been Italian quilted like its matching tie-back, but in which case it should be ladder-stitched into place on both sides by hand.

Plate 76, page 161, shows a similar use of a strip cut from a curtain fabric, but the tie-back is trapunto quilting this time and some velvet ribbon is incorporated with the print for the border and used for the piping on the tie-back.

70 The corner section of a quilted border on dupion curtains. 5 in (13 cm) wide

Plate 71 shows a printed border laid onto an unlined curtain.

71 A printed border pattern cut out and applied with a machine zig-zag stitch. The corner is mitred. 1½ in (4 cm) wide

WEAVING THREADS It is possible to lay these onto fabric with a narrow zigzag machine stitch, and build them up into a textural border. In Plate 72 a variety of threads are laid upon tweed.

72 Assorted natural coloured weaving threads couched onto tweed curtains with a machine zig-zag stitch. $2\frac{1}{2}$ in (6 cm) wide

PATCHWORK Very pleasant borders can be made from patchwork which can also be built up into attractive motifs.

CANVAS-WORK Borders of canvas-work can certainly be used but they do need to be mounted on a heavy material and to have the richness of interlining.

COMMERCIAL BORDERS It is not easy to find a wide choice of design or colour. Apart from this they are extremely expensive.

Measuring

Curtain Width
Base the measurements for the width of the curtains on the length of the curtain track, not on the width of the window.

The amount of fullness required in the curtains depends largely on the fabric, as thin unlined curtains will need more fullness than thicker interlined ones.

GATHERED HEADINGS Allow one and a half times to twice the length of the track.

PINCH PLEATS AND BOX PLEATS Allow two to two and a half times the length of the track.

PENCIL PLEATS AND MOST OF THE COMMERCIAL HEADINGS Two and a half to three times the length of the track is needed.

The instructions for using the commercial tape usually state how much fullness is necessary, and therefore the number of widths of fabric to buy can be estimated.

Do not skimp on the amount of fullness used as it really can ruin the curtains.

Decide on how many widths will be necessary for the whole track, then divide it up into the number of curtains required.

Curtain Length or Drop
CURTAINS SET INSIDE THE DEPTH OF THE WALL These should clear the windowsill by $\frac{1}{2}$ in (15 mm).

CURTAINS HUNG ON THE WALL IN FRONT OF THE SILL If they are required to hang to the length of the window, they should in fact end 2 in (5 cm) below the sill. Should the window be at an awkward height so that this point is exactly the halfway measurement on the wall, then make the curtains a few inches longer.

CURTAINS HUNG TO THE FLOOR These should clear the floor or carpet by no more than $\frac{1}{2}$ in (15 mm).

CURTAINS HUNG ACROSS A DOORWAY Make sure these break the floor by at least an inch (2.5 cm); otherwise they defeat their purpose of being draught excluders.

To any of the above measurements add an allowance for turnings on the hem and the heading. Between 5 and 9 in (13–23 cm) inclusive is normally allowed.

When cutting patterned fabric the curtain should be planned so that a pattern finishes on the bottom edge of the curtain. The pattern must match at every seam, and one curtain to the next. To cater for this an extra whole pattern repeat must be allowed for on every 'drop' of curtain cut out.

The measurement for the length of fabric is then multiplied by the number of widths required, to give the total measurement for purchase.

Order of Work

This resumé is intended to help when making curtains, but please do check the detailed methods in the following sections before making the first pair.

1. Plan the position and length of curtain track.
2. Decide on the length of the curtains.
3. Decide on the weight of the fabric, type of heading, and the necessary fullness.
4. Estimate the total fabric, interlining, lining and heading tape required.
5. Cut out the fabric, interlining and lining.
6. Work embroidery on individual widths.
7. Join widths and half widths as necessary for each curtain. Snip selvedges on seams and cut off selvedge on side hems.
8. Work embroidery over any seams.
9. Lay interlining onto the fabric and attach with rows of locking-stitch.
10. Fold and herringbone fabric to interlining on side hems.
11. Lay lining onto interlining and attach with rows of locking-stitch.
12. Fold, pin, tack and ladder-stitch side hems of the lining to the curtain.
13. Fold, pin and tack tops of curtains.
14. Apply heading tape or make headings.
15. Put in hooks and hang for two or three days to allow the curtains to drop.
16. Turn up hem and herringbone onto interlining. Insert weights if necessary.
17. Mitre corners of hem and side hems.
18. Turn up hem of lining to its wrong side.
19. Work buttonhole bars between each seam of the fabric and the lining on the hem-line, to stop them ballooning apart in a draught.

Cutting

Cut plain fabric to the grain of the material. If possible pull out a thread to get a straight line for cutting.

Cut patterned fabric to the pattern and not to the grain, as it is often badly printed and not on the grain.

Mark out each length of curtain, being sure to match the pattern, pinning the lengths and marking the cutting line with tailor's chalk and the metre or yard stick. Re-check all measurements before finally cutting out the curtains.

Mark the top of each length of fabric with a coloured tack as it comes off the bolt to make absolutely certain that each length hangs the correct way. This is especially important with something like velvet.

Headings

Gathered Headings
The commercial 1-in (3-cm) pocketed tape gives a simple gathered heading that is suitable for use under pelmets or valances where the heading does not show (Fig. 185).

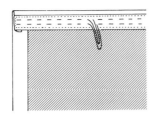

Fig. 185. Simple gathered heading

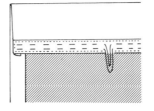

Fig. 186. A small frill above the heading tape

It can also be used to give a small frill above the heading on lightweight lined or unlined curtains (Fig. 186). If the frill should need some extra stiffening a strip of Vilene can be inserted into the fold behind the tape to the top edge of the frill.

MACHINING ON THE TAPE The top edge of the fabric is folded over to the required depth and pressed.

The tape is laid over the raw edge and tacked or pinned into position.

The tape requires $\frac{3}{4}$ in (2 cm) turning at each end to neaten it. The cords are folded in as well and a back-stitch or two is worked through each cord onto the tape to make sure that it cannot slip out.

The tape is machined along the first end, along the top of the tape, and down the second end. The curtain is then removed from the machine, and the lower edge of the tape is machined in the same direction. This prevents any puckering of the fabric on the tape on the right side, which can easily happen.

The curtain and tape is then pulled up into gathers by the cords in the middle of the curtain, or one third and two thirds along on a very wide curtain. By doing this the long cord ends hang in the middle of the curtain, and no ends appear sticking out at the sides. Secondly, as the cord ends are in loops there is no danger of them running back and the ends being lost in the tape, when the gathers are loosened off for washing or cleaning.

Pinch-Pleated and Pencil-Pleated Headings

There is a wide selection of pocketed tapes available on the market, and one can be found to give the right pleat to suit each weight of fabric.

The pleating is formed either by simply drawing up the cords of the tape or by inserting single, double, or triple hooks into pockets on the tape. The hooks are available for each type of tape and come in various lengths to give stiffness to the different heights of heading.

The tape is sewn on by the same method as for gathered headings.

A much wider range of headings can be made by hand, using a variety of pleating and smocking methods. All the headings must be stiffened by Vilene or something similar before beginning otherwise the heading will not be firm enough and will flop. The pleating having been completed, a plain heading tape is sewn on the back by hand and the hooks then stitched into position.

Tab Heading (Fig. 187)

This heading is used with a pole for hanging flat curtains to be used decoratively, for bed-heads, or as café curtains.

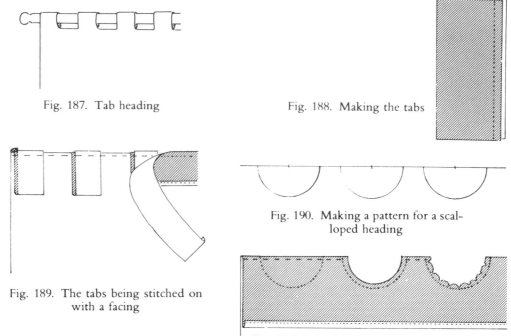

Fig. 187. Tab heading

Fig. 188. Making the tabs

Fig. 190. Making a pattern for a scalloped heading

Fig. 189. The tabs being stitched on with a facing

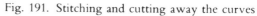

Fig. 191. Stitching and cutting away the curves

TAB For a tab 2 in (5 cm) wide and 9 in (23 cm) long, cut a strip of fabric 5 in (13 cm) wide and 10 in (25 cm) long. This allows ½-in (15-mm) turnings.

Fold the strip in half lengthwise, right side to right side, pin and machine the seam with ½-in (15-mm) turnings leaving the ends open (Fig. 188).

Pull the tab through to the right side and press flat so that the seam lies in the middle of the wrong side.

The tabs are folded in half and laid equidistantly along the top of the curtain.

For a small café curtain they are stitched to the top of the curtain with a facing (Fig. 189).

For a larger curtain the tabs will need to be interlined with a medium-weight Vilene, and a strip of the same Vilene laid against the wrong side of the curtain before machining on the tabs and the facing.

Do cut strips of paper to check the width of tab that looks best for a particular curtain, and the length of tab required to go round the pole and to look reasonable with the length of curtain.

Scalloped Headings (Colour Plate C)

This heading is another one that shows up to advantage when hung flat, or with very little fullness. The heading must be interlined unless the material is very firm.

Cut out the pattern in paper using a pair of compasses or a saucer (Fig. 190).

Fold the top of the curtain fabric over to the depth of 3 in (7 cm) right sides to right sides, and trace the pattern onto the fabric with tailor's chalk.

Stitch round the curves, cut away the surplus material leaving $\frac{1}{4}$-in (5-mm) turnings, snip these carefully so that the scallops will turn through without puckers (Fig. 191).

Turn the fabric through to the right side and press the scallops accurately so that the seam lies on the edge.

Tack and slip-stitch the hem of the facing to the fabric of the curtain.

Sew on the rings.

Unlined Curtains (Plate 73)

Cut out the curtains. Join the widths or half widths together as necessary. Press the seams open, snipping into the selvedge to prevent it pulling on the seam.

73 Calico bathroom curtains sprayed over a stencil to give the background pattern. The motif is reversed in the two positions

SIDE HEMS Cut off the selvedge on the side hems. This prevents puckering when the curtain is washed.

Make a 1-in (3-cm) double hem (Fig. 192). This can be sewn on the machine with a blind hem-stitch or slip-stitched by hand. A straight machine-stitched hem gives a very cheap-looking finish.

The double hem is needed to give extra strength to the edge, and to prevent any raw hem turning giving a shadow when hung against the light.

If a border is being applied and the fabric is reversible then an excellent finish is obtained by turning the hem over to the right side and laying the raw edge under the border. The corner of the side and bottom hem will need to be mitred.

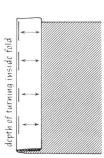

Fig. 192. A double hem on the side of an unlined curtain

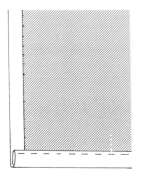

Fig. 193. Turning up a double hem on the bottom edge of a curtain

If the fabric has a definite right and wrong side, and the hem has to be turned to the wrong side, the hem can still be attached with the stitch line of the border. This prevents a second row of stitching marking the fabric.

This deep side hem of double fabric does give extra strength to the edge which will be handled every day when the curtains are drawn.

HEADING Make the chosen heading.

BOTTOM HEM The bottom edge is turned up to give a 2-in (5-cm) double hem (Fig. 193), stitched in the same way as the side hem. This width hem does add weight to the curtains and helps them to hang well.

Lined Curtains

Thin Fabric

Cut out the curtain fabric allowing 2-in (5-cm) turnings on each side hem, and $2\frac{1}{2}$ in (6 cm) on the bottom hem.

The lining is cut $1\frac{1}{2}$ in (4 cm) narrower than the fabric on each side hem, and $\frac{1}{2}$ in (15 mm) shorter on the bottom hem.

Lay the lining onto the fabric placing right sides to right sides and pin up the side hems. Machine ½-in (15-mm) seams from the top of the curtain to within 5 in (13 cm) of the bottom edge. Always machine curtains from the top downwards.

Press the seams and turn the curtain so that the right side is outside. Adjust the lay of the curtain to give 1½-in (4-cm) hems of fabric on both side hems. Pin into position and press.

HEADING Make the chosen heading.

BOTTOM HEM Turn the fabric up to the wrong side to give a 2-in (5-cm) hem with ½-in (15-mm) turning, and slip-stitch invisibly.

Turn the lining hem up to the wrong side so that the bottom edge is ½ in (15 mm) shorter than the curtain edge. The lining hem can be machined rather than sewn by hand if preferred.

74 Curtain border pattern with machine-applied shapes, and couched threads. *Mollie Picken*

The lining hem must always overlap the curtain hem, otherwise the light shines through the gap between the lining and the hem and appears a different colour.

The bottom of the side hem can be slip-stitched together.

Thick Fabric
Cut out the curtain fabric allowing 2½-in (6-cm) turnings on each side hem and the bottom hem. The lining is cut 2 in (5 cm) narrower than the fabric on each side hem, and ½ in (15 mm) shorter on the bottom hem.

Lay the fabric flat on a table and turn the side hems in 2½ in (6 cm) onto the wrong side and catch-stitch (Fig. 194) them onto the fabric.

BOTTOM HEM Turn up the bottom hem 2½ in (6 cm) onto the wrong side, mitre the corners, and catch-stitch the hem onto the fabric.

LINING Lay the lining onto the fabric wrong sides to wrong sides. Pin together down the centre from the top to the bottom. Fold back one half of the lining, and work a row of locking-stitch from the top to within 6 in (15 cm) of the bottom hem (Fig. 195). This is to keep the lining and fabric together, and to prevent the lining dropping. The stitch must be worked in a thread to match the curtain fabric and kept loose so that it is invisible and does not pull the threads of the curtain fabric.

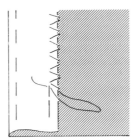

Fig. 194. Catch-stitching a hem

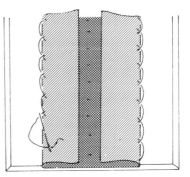

Fig. 195. Attaching the lining to the curtain fabric with locking stitch

The locking-stitch is worked at 16-in (40-cm) intervals and whenever possible on seam turnings.

Turn in the side hems ½ in (15 mm) and ladder-stitch them to the fabric side hems.

HEADING Make the chosen heading.

BOTTOM HEM OF LINING The bottom hem of the lining is turned up 2 in (5 cm) onto its own wrong side and sewn by hand or machine.

The curtains hang very much better if the two hems are made up independently and not hemmed together.

Interlined Curtains

Cut out the curtain fabric and interlining allowing $2\frac{1}{2}$-in (6-cm) turnings on each side hem and the bottom hem. The lining is cut 2 in (5 cm) narrower than the fabric and interlining on each side hem, and $\frac{1}{2}$ in (15 mm) shorter on the bottom hem.

Lay the curtain fabric flat on a table with the wrong side uppermost. Lay the interlining on top matching the edges. Interlock the interlining into position.

Using the fabric and interlining as one piece of material continue making up as for LINED CURTAINS—Thick Fabric page 158.

Pelmets

Pelmets were originally used to cover up the curtain rails and the curtain headings, but they do very much more than this. In high-ceilinged rooms pelmets play an important part to give interest and to help the proportions of the whole wall.

They can be made by draping a length of fabric over a pole (Fig. 196), or by cutting and sewing it to give this appearance.

The flat tailored pelmets (Fig. 197) can look very good made up with patchwork or quilting or even the two combined. Embroidered and applied motifs, borders or just braided edges can all be most attractive.

It needs to be remembered when working on the designs that they are always seen from a distance, and at above eye level.

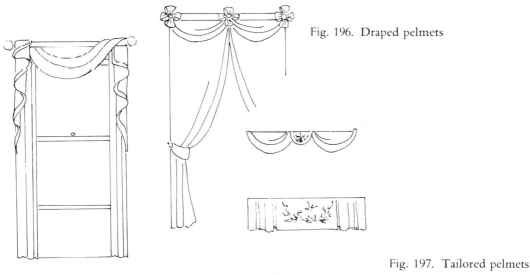

Fig. 196. Draped pelmets

Fig. 197. Tailored pelmets

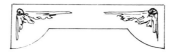

To Make Up

The embroidered fabric is cut to the length of the pelmet plus the return at either end and turnings all round.

The depth of the pelmet depends on the length of the curtains and the height of the room. It is advisable to make a paper pattern of the pelmet to see how it looks.

Buckram or pelmet Vilene can be used to back the pelmets. As these are rather hard an interlining should be used.

PELMET VILENE The interlining and then the fabric can be turned onto the wrong side of the Vilene and herringboned firmly into position.

BUCKRAM This is made of a heavy canvas stiffened with glue so the interlining, and then the fabric with deeper turnings can be attached in the following way:

Place the buckram in position on the interlining, and starting at the top edge damp the buckram slightly with a sponge, fold the turnings of the interlining over onto the buckram and press with a hot iron. Continue all the way round the pelmet snicking into the turnings on the curves, and trimming away the surplus interlining on the corners.

Repeat the process for the fabric, having first pinned it firmly in position and having checked that it is correctly centred and lying on the straight grain. Slip-stitch the corners, and apply any trimmings by stab-stitching right through the backing.

Lay on the lining, turn the edges under and slip-stitch into position.

POCKETED STRIP Using 1–1½ in (3–4 cm) width heading tape make the pocketed strip for drawing-pinning the pelmet to the pelmet board.

Lay the tape along the top edge of the pelmet on the wrong side, and turn in ½ in (15 mm) at each end. Back-stitch the ends and bottom edge of the tape with a strong thread onto the pelmet. Make sure that you go through the backing but do not go through the fabric. Then stitch the tape down every 4 in (10 cm) to form pockets (Fig. 198). Push a drawing pin through tape in each pocket and attach to pelmet board.

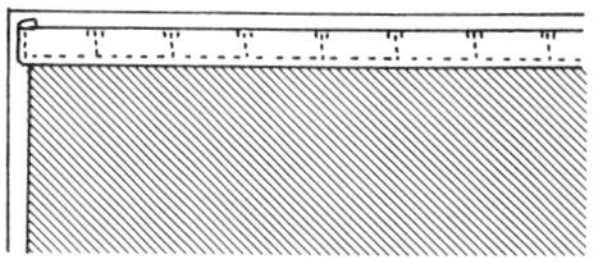

Fig. 198. Pocketed heading tape for a pelmet

Tie-Backs

By holding back the curtains into neat swags, tie-backs help more light to penetrate the room, and at the same time soften the line of a straight drop of fabric. Either fact can add to the decorative quality in the room.

This small piece of fabric is a pleasant use for embroidery and a technique can be chosen to suit the surrounding furnishings, either using the same fabric as the curtains or a complementary one.

75 A strip of patterned fabric used as a border on a curtain. Italian quilting has been worked on the tie-back. 4 in (10 cm) wide.

76 A strip of patterned fabric used as a border on a curtain with a 1½ in (4 cm) velvet ribbon on one edge. The tie-back is worked in trapunto quilting and piped with the same green ribbon. The tie-back is 4¾ in (12 cm) wide.

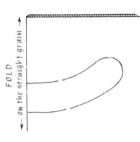

FOLD on the straight grain

Fig. 199. Pattern for curved tie-back

77 Canvas worked tie-backs with additional surface stitchery. 27 in × 4½ in (69 cm × 11 cm).
Joan Broughton

Pattern

A tie-back comes in two main shapes: straight (Plates 75 and 76) and curved (Plate 77 and Fig. 199).

To make the pattern cut out the required shape in calico to try round the curtains. Do not make it too tight, otherwise it will crease the curtains.

To Make Up

Vilene or tailor's canvas make a good interlining. Pelmet Vilene is a little too rigid for the purpose.

Cut out the pattern.

Cut out the interlining to the pattern with no extra turnings.

Cut out the embroidered fabric with ¾-in (2-cm) turnings all round.

Cut out the lining with ½-in (15-mm) turnings all round.

Bump or wadding should be used if the embroidery technique calls for some additional softening against the Vilene. This is cut to the size of the pattern.

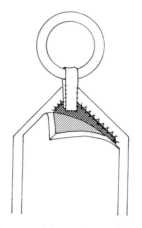

Fig. 200. Attaching a ring to the tie-back

Lay the bump and interlining onto the wrong side of the fabric. Fold over the fabric turnings and herringbone into position onto the interlining. Mitre the two ends.

Attach the brass or wooden rings by loops of folded matching fabric, which are firmly sewn to the interlining at each end (Fig. 200).

Lay on the lining, fold under the edges, pin and slip-stitch into place.

CHAPTER SIX

Blinds

Designing the Blind

Blinds are a very practical window covering especially in bathrooms and kitchens where they take up little space, and are less likely to collect the grease and dust.

Being a flat area they are an exciting project for the embroiderer. However, as blinds have to be very flat to roll successfully, techniques with the least texture are the most practical. Flat machine embroidery using free or fixed stitchery makes a good flat finish.

Cut-work should be machined round with a close zig-zag stitch before cutting to avoid distortion. The spraying that follows will prevent any fraying.

Appliqué using thin fabrics and Bondaweb to keep it flat and bonded to the background is an attractive possibility (Plate 78). Simple edge treatments should be used to avoid any bulk.

78 A blind with a deep applied border. *From a screen print by Trotman Foster*

Counted thread techniques are well worth while experimenting with.

Shadow work can be very effective, as long as it is kept very flat.

It is really more practical if the main embroidery is restricted to the lower 10 in (25 cm) so that the major part of the blind rolls up neatly. It looks very effective if the weight of the design is on the bottom edge of the blind, gradually drifting away as it goes up the blind.

It is an advantage when the design can break the hard straight edge of the bottom (Plate 79). Plate 80 shows a printed fabric border that has been faced and applied to give a scalloped finish. This could well have been an embroidered strip.

79 A blind with a border of applied quilted mushrooms

80 A printed scalloped border applied to the blind below the batten to give a broken edge

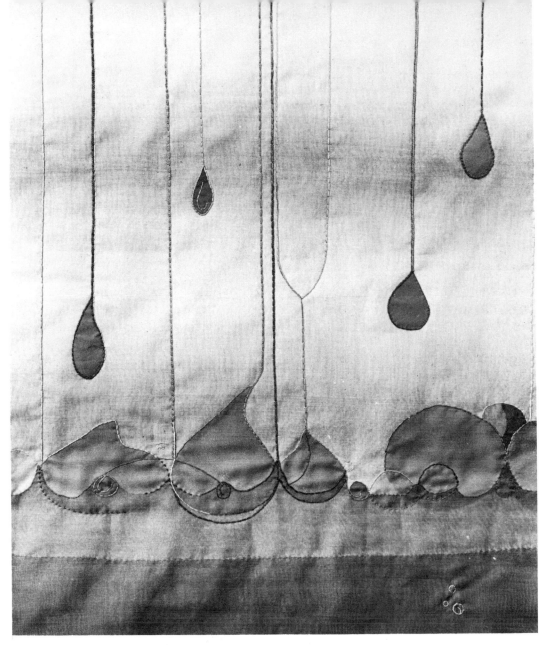

81 A blind made up of layers of organdie and organzas

If a window has a dreary outlook, for example a staircase window may look out onto a blank wall, the blind can be kept down all the time so that the problem about rolling does not arise. Plate 81 is worked in layers of organdie and organza so that a back light is an important part of its design.

It is important to be very careful about the handling of the embroidery threads on the back of the blind. Any thread passing from one point to another will show up as a shadow in daylight, and may spoil the design. Similarly all loose ends must be carefully worked in and cut off.

Tools and Materials

Fabric

HOLLAND The traditional material for blinds, it is not at all sympathetic to embroidery. However, it is available in a good range of colours so it would be possible to apply a contrasting embroidered border below the batten.

CLOSELY WOVEN COTTONS, CALICOS AND LINENS These are the main choice of fabrics for embroidered blinds. Once treated with a special spray for blinds, they stiffen up very well and can be wiped.

Avoid loosely woven fabrics and those that are thick and bulky, as they will not roll up well.

Blind Spray

The spray especially made for using on home-made blinds stiffens the fabric and provides a surface that can be wiped. There are several on the market and some are better than others.

Depending on the fabric, several coats will be required to get a satisfactory finish.

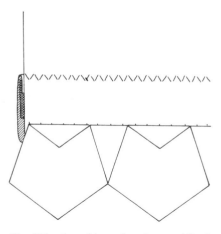

Fig. 201. Attaching a border to a blind

82 A tern worked in raised chain band and raised stem band on a sprayed background to make a long narrow blind

Roller Blind Kits
These are available from big stores selling furnishing fabrics. They are made in a range of sizes, and can be cut down to the exact measurement required.

They are complete with everything that is needed:

A wooden roller with a spring and a metal end cap
A second metal end cap to attach when the roller has been cut to size
Two metal brackets to carry the blind
Tacks for fixing the blind to the roller
A pull cord and acorn fitment (home-made cords and specially chosen china, glass or wooden beads can replace the commercial set to suit the embroidery)
A wooden batten to stiffen and to give weight to the bottom edge of the blind

Tools
A screwdriver, a small saw and a hammer for erecting the blind will be needed and, of course, normal sewing equipment with matching threads and a large pair of shears.

Order of work

1. Decide whether the blind is to be fixed on the wall, or inside the window recess on the window frame.
2. Measure the width required. If the kit cannot be bought in the exact size, then the next size up can be cut down to the required measurements.
3. Cut the wooden roller to the correct size to fit between the two brackets, following the manufacturer's instructions.
4. Cut the fabric to the width of the roller plus 1 in (3 cm). The length of the fabric will be the height of the window plus 6–9 in (15–23 cm) inclusive of turnings. The fabric must be cut accurately to the grain, and if that is out of true, use a set square to make sure that the blind is square, otherwise it will never roll up evenly.
5. Work the embroidery.
6. The blind will roll much better with raw side edges, and the spray will prevent any fraying. But if a hem is preferred turn in the surplus $\frac{1}{2}$ in (15 mm) both sides and machine from the top downwards with a zig-zag stitch. Press well.
7. At the bottom edge of the blind make a $1\frac{1}{2}$-in (4-cm) hem with $\frac{1}{2}$ in (15 mm) turned under (using 2 in (5 cm) in all), to make a casing for the batten. Machine the hem with a zig-zag stitch.
   If a border is to be attached, make the hem $\frac{1}{2}$ in (15 mm) deeper so that the border can be ladder-stitched right through the bottom fold, leaving room for the batten above it (Fig. 201). The batten is indicated by the darker shading at the left-hand end of the diagram.
8. Pin up the blind outside, so that it hangs flat, and spray evenly all over one side with the blind spray. Allow to dry. Spray the other side. Repeat as necessary until the blind is sufficiently stiff to roll well.

9. If the side edges are to be left raw, cut off the surplus $\frac{1}{2}$in (15 mm) each side.

10. Fix the top of the blind to the wooden roller as directed by the kit's instructions, making sure that it lies absolutely straight on the roller.

11. Cut the wooden batten to the width of the blind and insert it in the casing.

12. Either use the pull cord and acorn knob provided with the kit, or make a finger cord to compliment the embroidery and knot onto it a suitable bead. The fitment provided can then be screwed to the batten to hold the cord.

CHAPTER SEVEN

Book Covers

Designing the Book Cover

Book covers must be made suitable for their use like every other article. A cover to protect a treasured volume may not have the same requirements as one that has been made to cover a presentation copy for a specific occasion. On the other hand folders and loose-leaf covers which have been made to hold gardening tips or cookery recipes need a more serviceable finish, and may have a much simpler design.

When designing the cover lay out the whole piece and consider the front, spine and back panels together. Do remember that the front of the cover is the right hand section (Fig. 202).

Book covers fall into four main groups.

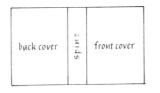

Fig. 202. Bookcover laid out ready to design the embroidery

Slip-On Covers (Plate 83)
These are embroidered according to their specific use and are made of thin, closely woven material. The cover encloses the bound book, but can be removed if wished. This does mean that it can be easily replaced if it gets dirty or worn, but it is permanent enough to give pleasure for a long time if treated carefully.

Close-Bound Covers (Plate 84)
These are the amateur's way of applying a permanent cover without regard to the bookbinder's skill, which is a separate craft in itself. The existing book cover is covered in a permanent fashion, without taking the binding to pieces which a bookbinder would do.

83 An initialled slip-on cover for a prayer book with appliqué and stitchery. *Valerie Harding*

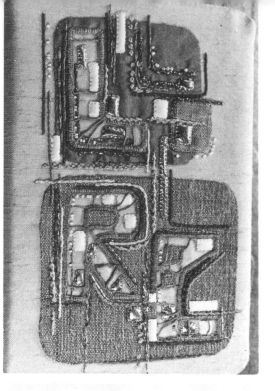

84 Two bibles with inlaid gold leather lettering. 6 in × 9¼ in (15 cm × 24 cm)

Professional Bound Covers (Colour Plate E)

There are very few people today who will handle the binding of books wholly or partially with embroidery. The results are beautiful, but only the very best of the embroiderer's skills should be entrusted to their time and effort.

Folders and Loose-Leaf Covers (Plate 85)

The covering boards can hold any mementoes, scraps or information, and they can be tailored to individual size and need.

They can be simply back and front boards, plain or hinged, tied together with a thong, lace or a pair of screws. Alternatively, they can have a built in back spine which limits the amount of information stored.

85 Hessian and canvas work combined to make a flat folder for gardening cuttings. *Valerie Harding*

Inserting a Contrasting Fabric or Technique

It is often required to insert a small piece of embroidery into a cover. This can give a very pleasing finish and make an interesting focal point.

Canvas-work is such a bulky technique that a much crisper finish is obtained if it is not used for the complete cover, but is joined or set into the cover.

There are four methods of construction.

Inset Behind Covered Card (Plate 86)

This method has been used for box lids and for bag flaps. A hole is cut in thick card to suit the design of the embroidery and the shape of the article. The fabric edge of the hole is either faced with matching material, or, if the fabric has a lot of stretch like panné velvet, jersey, suede or leather it can be taken through the hole and stretched cleanly over the edge of the card. It is then laced to the turnings of the outside edge.

86 A loose-leaf folder with a spine designed to hold the National Trust magazine. The design derived from oak leaves is gold-work and applied leathers on tweed. *Embroidery by Daphne Nicholson*

The embroidery is laced onto thin card and attached behind the hole. The whole front board can then be lined with a piece of thin card laced with lining fabric.

This method is only suitable for a cover or folder where card would be used for the interlining. Otherwise there would be two layers of card, the cover and the actual bookbinding and it would be far too thick and heavy.

Joining Canvas-work to Fabric

There are several ways of doing this. Three are shown in Plate 87.

(a) The canvas has a folded edge which is laid onto the fabric and an edge-stitch is worked.

(b) The canvas is left with a raw edge and is glued onto the fabric before the edge-stitch is worked.

(c) The fabric is folded and laid onto the canvas with a back-stitch.

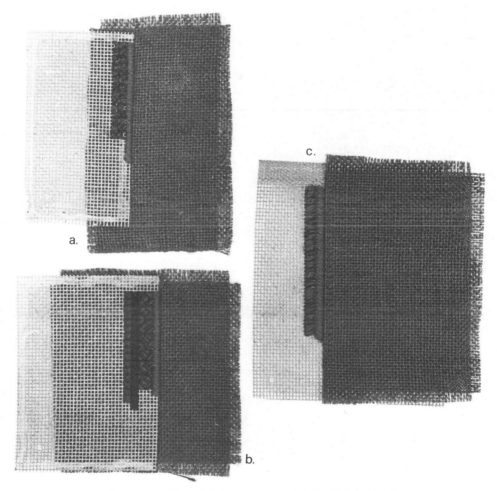

87 Three methods of joining canvas to fabric. *Valerie Harding*

88 An enlarged detail of transfer-type letters laid onto gaberdine for a cookery book

Lettering

The book or folder needs to be marked to show its contents. This information can either be given by a recognizable motif representing the subject, or by the use of lettering. The type of technique used depends on the fabric. Letters can be embroidered by hand or by machine and appliqued. If it is a felt or leather cover then they can be inlaid (Plate 84, page 170).

If a smooth, closely woven fabric has been selected, rub-on, transfer-type letters can be used. Two layers of letters are needed to cover the threads properly and they should be sealed with the matt spray sealer made specifically for this purpose. Do test an off-cut of the fabric with the letters and the sealer to make sure that it does not stain and gives a satisfactory result before tackling the cover. The disadvantage of this excellent range of lettering is that it only comes in black and this may not suit the design (Plate 88). The rub-off letters give a very neat finish but they only have a limited use as they would look out of place with anything more decorative than simple applied motifs.

Tools and Materials

Fabric
The fabric needs to be closely woven, firm, and no more than medium weight. Heavy textured fabrics are just too bulky. A great deal depends on the size of the book, as the fabric must look proportionally correct. Lining material needs to be thin and firm.

Normal Sewing Equipment
Good scissors, accurate tape measure, matching sewing thread to the selected fabric. Tailor's chalk etc.
Sharp pencils, set square and steel rule.

Marker Ribbons
Narrow widths of ribbon can be used for markers. They should be neatly attached to the book cover at the top of the spine. The ends can be hemmed and decorated. If a cut

end is preferred, a thin layer of clear nail varnish should be painted along the cut edge to prevent it fraying.

Requirements for Slip-on Covers

Calico Can be used as an interlining.

Medium-weight Vilene May be needed to interline to give the fabric extra body.

Bondaweb A Vilene product which bonds two fabrics together, making a firm finish. This could give the required finish on some designs.

Card Medium or thick card is used as an interlining for slip-covers being made for paperbacks, depending on their size.

Shirring elastic Used to lie between the pages of a paperbacked volume to keep the spine of the cover neatly in place.

Requirements for Close-bound Covers

Glue Rubber solution and stick glue are both useful.

Crochet Cotton A fine one is exellent for lacing the fabric over card.

Padding Thin felt or wadding may be needed on the card.

Calico For interlining.

End-papers The nicest available papers always add interest. Homemade or bought marbled papers are a traditional pattern.

Requirements for Folders and Loose-leaf Covers

Glue Rubber solution and stick glue are both useful.

Card Thick card is used in the basic construction of these covers. Thin card is used to interline the lining of these covers.

Crochet Cotton A fine one for lacing the fabric over card.

Padding Thin felt or wadding may be needed on the card.

A Punch To make holes for the ties.

A Tool For inserting metal eyelets into belts.

Screws Also extension rods for lengthening the screws, to carry the paper in the folder.

Order of Work for the Slip-on Cover

This kind of cover involves more technique than the other types and the following list may be helpful. However, do not start work until you have read the full instructions.

1. Choose the fabric.
2. Make the paper pattern and mark it on the fabric.
3. Work the embroidery.

4. Cut out the fabric and lining.
5. Interline if necessary.
6. Fold in the turnings on the back flap edge of the fabric, and of the lining. Press.
7. Lay the lining onto the fabric right side to right side and pin. Machine right round, leaving open the back flap edge. Press edges, snick into angles and trim surplus fabric from the corners.
8. Turn through to the right side. Tack and press edges.
9. Ladder-stitch the fabric and lining together on the back flap edge.
10. Place the cover round the book, pin the flaps to the cover.
11. Ladder-stitch the joins.
12. Push spine tabs into position.

Slip-on Covers (Plate 89)

Measuring
The book must be measured in the closed position.

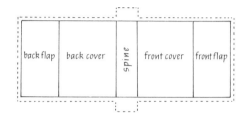

Fig. 203. The pattern laid out with turnings marked

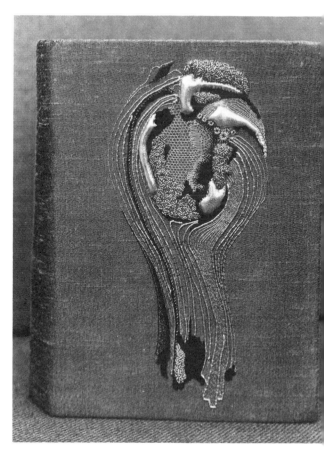

89 A slip-on bible cover with gold-work on silk.
Valda Cowie

WIDTH This is measured from the top back corner, across the back, round the spine, across the front to the other top corner. If the cover is being made in canvas-work an extra $\frac{1}{2}$in (15 mm) should be added to the total measurement to allow for the thickness of the canvas, the wool and the lining.

HEIGHT This is measured at the edge of the spine on the front cover. If the cover is being made in canvas-work an extra $\frac{1}{4}$in (5 mm) should be added.

Pattern

Make a paper pattern to these measurements and add on the extra width needed for the flaps which hold the front and back covers. The flaps can be one or two thirds of the width of the cover. Mark the position where the flaps fold, and the edges of the spine on the pattern.

To Make Up

Cut out the fabric and a matching thin lining, allowing $\frac{1}{2}$-in (15-mm) turnings all round, and 3 in (7 cm) on the top and bottom edge of the spine (Fig. 203).

Using a calico backing on the frame, work the embroidery.

For a silk, dupion, or similar weight fabric cut the calico backing to the size of the pattern and use it as the interlining.

For a firm material trim the calico away close to the embroidery.

Fold the back flap turning onto the calico and catch-stitch it into position.

If an interlining is being used, catch-stitch it on the other three sides invisibly. Press, taking care not to press the embroidery.

Turn in the lining turning on the back flap edge and press.

Lay the lining onto the cover right sides to right sides. Pin into position (Fig. 204).

Stitch round by machine leaving the back flap edge open.

Snick into the angles with great care, and trim surplus material away from corners (Fig. 205). Press edges.

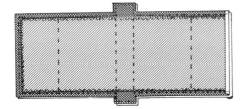

Fig. 204. The cover with interlining, laid onto the lining right sides to right sides and stitched. Tacks mark the fold lines

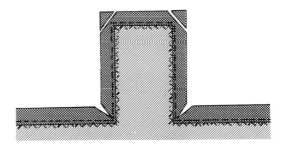

Fig. 205. Snipping into the corners and cutting away surplus material on the turnings

Turn through to the right side, tack the edges and press.

Ladder-stitch the fabric and lining together on the back flap edge.

Fold the cover round the book, which must be in the closed position, and pin the flaps to the front and back covers at the top and bottom edges.

Ladder-stitch these edges together, picking up the fabric and not the lining. It is probably easier to do this on the book rather than in the hand.

To remove the slip-on cover the book must be folded right back (Fig. 206). The cover is replaced in the same manner.

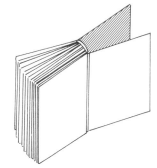

Fig. 206. The book folded right back to put on and take off a slip-on cover

When the cover is finally put on, the long tabs at the top and bottom of the spine are pushed down the back of the spine. Make sure that they are lying flat by using a round-ended knife to push them down.

If the fabric is thick or bulky it should not be used for the flaps as the book will not shut properly. Thin lining should be joined on at the front and back edges to make the flaps, and then made up as before.

The slip-on cover can be made with even deeper flaps which must be ladder-stitched to the cover whilst it is in position on the book. It is semi-permanent and does fit more snugly. It is advisable still to line the cover as otherwise there is a danger of untidy raw corners at the edge of the spine.

The cover can be made without the spine extensions to tuck in, but the fit is not as good.

Should an embroidery technique be used which requires extra tension to keep it in shape, the flaps should be as deep as possible and made of lining laced over thin card. This will keep the edge seams of the cover straight and neat.

Slip-On Cover for Paperbacks
For this type of cover the interlining for the front and back cover is made of card, which is cut to the size of the paper cover, and the fabric laced over it (Fig. 207).

If canvas-work is being used it will need to be worked $\frac{1}{4}$ in (5 mm) larger than the card in both directions for both the front and back cover.

A strip of Vilene is used to interline the spine.

A thin lining is laid over the whole of the inside of the cover and ladder-stitched into position. Deep flaps are then made by stitching and turning out a double piece of lining (Fig. 208).

Trim the corners, press, turn through to the right side. Press.

Pin and ladder-stitch the flaps onto the covers.

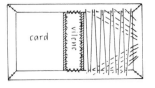

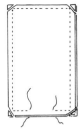

Fig. 207. Lacing the fabric over card for the front and back covers

Fig. 208. Double material stitched ready to turn through to make a flap

It will be noted that there are no spine extension pieces on this cover. This is because the spine of a paperback is glued to the paper edges, and there is therefore nowhere to tuck the fabric extension.

90 A patchwork book cover to suit a specified volume. *Valerie Harding*

If it is a thick book, shirring elastic can be inserted between the lining and the fabric at the top to run the length of the spine and to be fixed again at the bottom. It is then laid between the leaves of the book to keep the cover taut to the spine.

Three or four threads, equally spaced along the spine, can be used for a big book.

Close-Bound Covers

The cover is laced round the hard cover of the book then new fly papers are inserted.

If a richer finish is required a very thin layer of wadding can be lightly glued onto the outside of the binding before covering.

Measure the book over the padding, as for the Slip-on Cover.

Pattern

Make the pattern to the measurements, and mark the position of the edges of the spine. Allow 1-in (3-cm) turnings all round, and 3 in (7 cm) on top and bottom edges of the spine.

To Make Up

Making sure that the grain is straight to the edge of the book, pin or clip the fabric to hold it in place, with the book in the closed position.

Mitre the corners and lace the fabric from top to bottom, and at an angle to hold the side edges (Fig. 209).

Lacing can be replaced by glueing but it is difficult to let the glue dry under pressure without damaging the embroidery, and lacing is really more efficient.

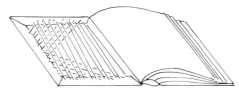

Fig. 209. Lacing the fabric over the hard cover of a book

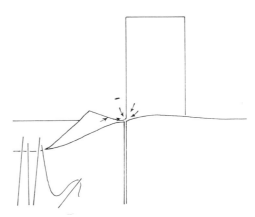

Fig. 210. Applying a little glue to the snipped-in corner of the spine to prevent fraying

When snipping into the corners of the spine (Fig. 210) a little glue can be applied to the edges to prevent them fraying. Be careful to only snip into the angles as the stage is reached for folding the fabric, because it is very easy to mis-judge and cut too far.

The spine extensions are kept in position by putting a little rubber solution on their wrong side before pushing them down into the spine with a round-headed knife.

A thin layer of calico is glued over the lacing to the edge of the fabric to stop the lacing thread marking the new end papers.

Cut the end papers out of suitable paper. Each one is a folded piece of paper, right sides inside, cut to the size of the paper leaves in the book.

One half is glued over the lacing on the cover and pushed well into the spine crease. The second half is glued to the first page. It is often easier to set the end paper to the page first, glue and paper clip it into position before setting the second half onto the inside of the cover.

Lay a sheet of greaseproof paper between the folded end papers, and the next pair of pages, and allow to dry with the book in the closed position.

Folders and Loose-Leaf Covers

These are made of a back and front cover with a hinged strip to carry the thong, laces, or screw fasteners. A back spine can be made into the folder, tying the front and back covers together.

It is perfectly practical to use a heavier fabric for this type of cover.

To Make Up
Using thick card, cut out the front and back cover to the size required.

The hinge strip is cut in thick card to the same height as the front and back cover and to a width of 1½ in–2 in (3 cm–5 cm) depending on overall size of cover (Fig. 211).

Fig. 211. Cutting the card for (a) back and front boards with hinged strips

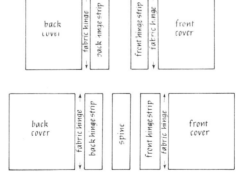

(b) back and front boards with hinged strips and a spine. The positions where the fabric hinges will lie are indicated

Cut the spine, if required, in thick card.

Pad the card with wadding or felt unless a thick fabric is being used, such as hessian, canvas, tweed or leather, when it is not a necessity.

Cut the fabric to cover the front and back boards.

Work the embroidery.

Pin the fabric on the straight grain to the card.

Mitre the corners and lace the fabric into place.

Cut the fabric to cover the two hinge strips.

SPINE If a spine is being made the hinge strips and spine are covered with one piece of fabric (Fig. 212). Because they cannot be laced a little stick glue is applied to the fabric and it is stuck into position on the card. The turnings are folded over and glued down.

If no spine is being used, then the two hinge strips are covered and laced separately.

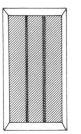

Fig. 212. The back and front hinge strips with the spine between them being covered by one piece of fabric

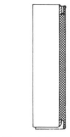

Fig. 213. Two strips of fabric being prepared for a hinge

HINGES To make the two hinges prepare four strips of the fabric 1½ in (4 cm) wide and the height of the cover plus ½-in (15-mm) turnings each end. Lay them in pairs with wrong sides to wrong sides. Fold in the turnings at each end and ladder-stitch (Fig. 213).

Lay the covered back cover and one covered hinge strip level, and ⅛ in (3 mm) apart with wrong sides uppermost.

Pin the hinge on top of the gap between them, and ladder-stitch into position down both long sides.

Repeat this with the covered front cover and the second covered hinge strip.

LINING Thin card is cut ⅛ in (3 mm) smaller all round to fit each of the hinge strips and the back and front covers independently.

Lace with lining fabric, interline if required.

Ladder-stitch onto the wrong side of each piece of the cover.

LINING FOR FOLDER WITH SPINE This is made up on thin card similar to the outside cover but ⅛ in (3 mm) smaller all round, and ladder-stitched into place.

FASTENINGS Punch holes in the hinge strip one-third of the way along from each end, to take the screw fittings and extension rods.

If thongs are being used the appearance is better if metal eyelets used for belts can be inserted.

If the holes have to be made with an old stiletto always make them from the outside. The holes are cleaner.

Plate 91 shows a loose-leaf cover which has contrasting hinge strip and corners. The corners and hinge strip fabric are laid on top of the grass paper that has been used for covering the front and back boards. The lining is simply paper glued into position in this basic version.

91 A loose-leaf cover with contrasting hinge strip and corners

A folder which is just a flat board and has no hinge strip is also a useful type to make (Plate 85, page 171). Although this is very simple from the construction point of view, it is a most attractive and decorative article which, being hessian and canvas-work, is practical and will stand up to a lot of hard wear.

Sources of Supply

Beckfoot Mill
Dept HC
Howden Road
Silsden
Keighley
West Yorkshire BD20 OMA

Terylene and polyester fillings and wadding.

Borovick Fabrics Ltd
16 Berwick Street
London W1V 4HP

A wide selection of all types of fabrics. A personal visit recommended.

Arthur Cordery
51 High Street
Shaftesbury
Dorset SP7 JBE

Curved needles.

Creative Beadcraft Ltd
Unit 26
Chiltern Trading Estate
Earl Howe Road
Holmer Green
High Wycombe
Buckinghamshire

Mail order. Beads, sequins, metal decorations, chains and lurex braids.

Ells and Farrier Ltd
5 Princes Street
Hanover Square
London W1

Personal shoppers only. Beads, sequins, etc. mail order now undertaken by Creative Beadcraft Ltd.

A. Godwin and Sons
59–61 Fisherton Street
Salisbury
Wiltshire

Assorted metal studs to use as feet on boxes and bags.

John Lewis
Oxford Street
London W1
and branches in most big cities

Courtelle wadding under own name 'Jonelle' in various weights.

Livingstone Textiles Co.
PO Box 5
St Michael's Lane
Bridport
Dorset

Cheesecloth, calicos, etc. and special offers in other fabrics.

MacCulloch and Wallis Ltd
25/26 Dering Street
London W1R OBU

Haberdashery, Vilenes, Bondaweb, Bondina, polyester boning. It is advisable to send for a catalogue.

Mace and Nairn
89 Crane Street
Salisbury
Wiltshire

All embroidery equipment and a very wide range of threads and traditional embroidery fabrics.

John P. Milner Ltd
Cilycwm
Llandovery
Dyfed SA20 0SS

Leathers — a wide selection. Send colour pattern and state measurement required.

Shades
517 Candlemas Lane
Beaconsfield
Bucks HP9 1AE

Threads, materials, and all sizes and types of curved needles.

Stephen Simpson Ltd
Avenham Road Works
Preston PR1 3UM

Metal threads and cords.

Whaleys (Bradford) Ltd
Harris Court
Great Horton
Bradford
Yorkshire

Good range of fabrics including water-soluble fabrics and those prepared for painting and dyeing.

T. C. Wiltshire
c/o Keith Bros
Houghton
Stockbridge SO20 6LP

Bookbinder.

Sources of Supply—U.S.A.

Materials available from each supplier are indicated by the following code:
B=Beads C=Cloth F=Felt S=Stuffing W=Webbing WB=Pre-assembled wooden boxes Y=Yarn

Y   Paternayan Bros., Inc.,
312 East 95th Street,
New York, N.Y. 10028

Y   Elsa Williams, Inc.,
West Townsend, MA 01474

F S WB Y   American Handicrafts/Merribee Needlearts and
Crafts Co.,
Box 9680,
Fort Worth, TX 76107

F S Y   Herrschners, Inc.,
Hoover Road,
Stevens Point, WI 54481

B F S Y   LeeWards,
1200 St. Charles Street,
Elgin, IL 60120

F S Y   Mary Maxim, Inc.,
2001 Holland Avenue,
Port Huron, MI 48060

B F S Y   Newark Dressmaker Supply Co.,
4616 Park Drive,
Bath PA 18014

Y   Erica Wilson Needle Works,
     717 Madison Avenue,
     New York, N.Y. 10021

F   Commonwealth Felt Co.,
     211 Congress Street,
     Boston, MA 02110

C Y   Fabric Cut-Aways,
     Arcadia, SC 29320

B F WB Hazel Pearson Handicrafts,
     16017 E. Valley Blvd.,
     City of Industry, CA 91744

W   Jim Dandy Sales,
     P.O. Box 30377,
     Cincinnati, OH 45230

WB   Adventures in Crafts,
     218 East 81 Street,
     New York, N.Y. 10028

WB   O-P Craft Co., Inc.,
     Sandusky, OH 44870

Bibliography

Harding, V., *Textures in Embroidery*, Batsford, 1977, 1985
Howard, C., *Embroidery and Colour*, Batsford, 1976, 1986
McNeill, M., *Pulled Thread*, Mills and Boon, 1971, 1986
McNeill, M., *Quilting for Today*, Mills and Boon, 1975
Russell, P., *Lettering for Embroidery*, Batsford, 1971, 1985
Erica Wilson's Embroidery Book, Faber and Faber, 1973

Glossary for U.S. Readers

Bias On the diagonal. On the bias
Blind Window blind, shade
Blind hemming Blind stitch
Blotting paper Blotter
Bonding card Board with sticky backing
Bump Cotton flannel. Outing flannel
Calico Unbleached canvas or muslin
Card Poster card—thick card is 3 mm thick
Clothes pegs Clip or spring pegs
Compass Drawing compass
Cords Twisted cords
Cotton sateen Curtain lining
Curtains Drapes
Cushion Pillow
Cushion pads Pillow forms
Downproof cambric 100–180 thread count, tightly woven cotton
Drawing pins Thumb tacks
Electric flex Electric cord
End papers (bookbinding) Decorative facing papers
Featherproof ticking Pillow ticking
Felt Wool felt
Flannel Wool flannel
Frame Embroidery frame
Frills Ruffles, ruching
Glue Adhesive
Gum Paper glue. White paste
Handbag Purse

Hardboard Masonite
Hessian Burlap, good quality
Iron Press
Jewellery Jewelry
Ladder-stitch A form of slip stitch
Millboard Mat board
Millinery wire Covered thin wire that holds its shape
Mount Mat
Nail varnish Nail polish
Pelmet Valance
Petersham ribbon Grosgrain ribbon
Piping Welting
Plait Braid
PVC Pacific cloth
PVA (Polyvinyl adhesive) water-soluble Sobo, etc.
Rubber solution Rubber cement
Saddlers Tack shop
Scrim Coarse woven hemp cloth, soft
Set square Triangle
Stanley Knife X-Acto Knife
Straight grain Straight of grain
Straw board Heavy card 3 mm thick
Studs Upholstery tacks
Tacking Basting
Vilene Pellon
Wadding Polyester batting
Webbing Upholsterers' webbing
Zip fastener Zipper